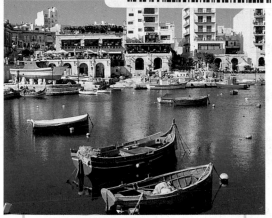

Essential
Malta &
Gozo

by Pat Levy

Pat Levy has written a number of
travel guidebooks, including the
AA *CityPack Hong Kong*.
Pat is now based in London, but
whenever time allows she can be found
busy gardening at her home in
West Cork in Ireland.

AA Publishing

7 TA GUNJU 1919

Above: *Riots flared in 1919 when four Maltese were shot by British troops – commemorative statue, St George's Square, Valletta*

Page 1: *Spinola Bay*

Page 5a: *Marsaxlokk fisherman*
5b: *Maltese dancer*

Page15a: *Ħaġar Qim*
15b: *Vessel from St Agatha's Catacombs*

Page 27a: *Republic Street, Valletta*
27b: *Mdina doorknocker*

Page 91a: *Gozo boat*
91b: *Automobile Association sign, Valletta*

Page 117a: *Tile decoration, Mdina*
117b: *Xlendi statue*

Find out more about AA Publishing and the wide range of services the AA provides by visiting our Web site at www.theaa.co.uk.

Written by Pat Levy

Edited, designed and produced by AA Publishing.
© The Automobile Association 1998
Maps © The Automobile Association 1998

Distributed in the United Kingdom by AA Publishing, Norfolk House, Priestley Road, Basingstoke, Hampshire, RG24 9NY.

A CIP catalogue record for this book is available from the British Library.

ISBN 0 7495 1624 0

Published by AA Publishing, a trading name of Automobile Association Developments Limited, whose registered office is Norfolk House, Priestley Road, Basingstoke, Hampshire, RG24 9NY.
Registered number 1878835.

Colour separation: BTB Digital Imaging Ltd, Whitchurch, Hampshire

Printed and bound in Italy by Printer Trento srl

Contents

About this Book

Essential *Malta and Gozo* is divided into five sections to cover the most important aspects of your visit to Malta and Gozo.

Viewing Malta and Gozo pages 5–14
An introduction to Malta and Gozo by the author.
Features of Malta and Gozo
Essence of Malta and Gozo
The Shaping of Malta and Gozo
Peace and Quiet
Famous of Malta and Gozo

Top Ten pages 15–26
The author's choice of the Top Ten places to see in Malta and Gozo, each with practical information.

What to See pages 27–90
The four main areas of Malta and Gozo, each with its own brief introduction and an alphabetical listing of the main attractions.
Practical information
Snippets of 'Did You Know…' information
5 suggested walks
3 suggested tours
2 features

Where To… pages 91–116
The best places to eat and drink, stay, shop, take the children and be entertained.

Practical Matters pages 117–24
A highly visual section containing essential travel information.

Maps
All map references are to the individual maps found in the What to See section of this guide.
For example, the Palace of the Grand Masters in Valletta has the reference ✛ 35D4 – indicating the page on which the map is located and the grid square in which the palace is to be found. A list of the maps that have been used in this travel guide can be found in the index.

Prices
Where appropriate, an indication of the cost of an establishment is given by **£** signs: **£££** denotes higher prices, **££** denotes average prices, while **£** denotes lower charges.

Star Ratings
Most of the places described in this book have been given a separate rating:

✪✪✪   Do not miss
✪✪   Highly recommended
✪   Worth seeing

Viewing
Malta & Gozo

Pat Levy's
Malta & Gozo

Mediterranean Crossroads
If the Mediterranean Sea had a central crossroads, Malta would mark the spot. Sicily is just over 90km to the north, North Africa under 300km to the south. Spain and Gibraltar 1,820km to the west, and Egypt 1,750km to the east are roughly equidistant. Malta itself is made up of two main islands, Malta and Gozo, separated by a mere 8km, with the largely uninhabited, tiny island of Comino in between.

The islands of Malta and Gozo are set right in the middle of the Mediterranean and at the narrowest place, thus smack on an ancient and turbulent crossroads. In striking contrast to their small size, their historic legacy is immense. Once the Romans came for precious honey. Today, as you gaze at honey-coloured walls this sense of age is all enveloping. The catalogue of fearsome invaders, from ancient times to World War II, has made Malta's language, food and architecture an enticing mix of European, Arabian and British influences. Yet, unbelievably, Malta's culture is distinctively its own.

Here are prehistoric monuments built 1,000 years before the pyramids, Roman ruins and the truly awesome defensive works of the Knights of Malta, the latter largely unaltered and part of an extraordinary wealth of architecture. Agriculture and fishing are important, but this is a busy working place with good shopping, numerous markets and a lively tourist life.

But remember: in these often overlooked islands time can come adrift. A spell may be cast by the sun and the deep turquoise sea, the scent of citrus groves on the wind, the fields of wildflowers in the spring, and the fresh Mediterranean food served alfresco with a glass of wine. Brightly painted *luzzu* bob in the harbours, and then there are the endearingly ancient cars and buses – each often carrying its own little shrine, perhaps reflecting the sometimes perilous driving conditions, red telephone boxes, and families enjoying the evening stroll or *passeggiata*. Smaller and more verdant Gozo and minute Comino enhance even further the feeling of a place apart. Once you relax into a pace of life that is full of vitality, but a few steps back in time, you may stay longer than you had intended.

Yet it is the islanders themselves one recalls with affection. They are engagingly affable: if you ask directions, you may be invited in for a cup of tea. This is a rare place where the Mediterranean sun is more than equalled by the sun that shines 'from the heart'.

Painting on the prow of a luzzu is an ancient tradition that predates St Paul's arrival on Malta

Features of Malta & Gozo

Size
Malta's longest distance from the southeast to the northwest is 27km and the widest point from east to west is 14km. Gozo is 14km long and 7km at its widest.

Population
Some 330,000 Maltese live on the island of Malta and 26,000 live on Gozo (calling themselves Gozitans, not Maltese). Malta ranks fourth in the world in terms of population density.

Diaspora
An estimated 300,000 Australians are of Maltese origin. World-wide the figure is put at over 1 million.

Government
A constitutional republic with its members of parliament elected every five years by universal suffrage.

Languages
Malti and English are the official languages. Italian is widely spoken, German to a lesser extent.

Religion
Most Maltese are Roman Catholics.

Cultural Influence
The British influence reveals itself in the colour of the telephone boxes, the popularity of afternoon tea and bacon and eggs for breakfast, and the daily use of English.

The Italian influence is evident in the popularity and prevalence of pasta and pizza dishes. Young people follow Italian trends in fashionable dress, and Italian television channels are broadcast.

The Turkish influence may still be seen in the popularity of Turkish Delight, a jelly-like, sweet dessert. The spectacular walls and bastions of Valletta may also, in one sense, be attributed to the Turks, for they were built to keep them out.

The Arab influence shows itself in the language, Malti, 70 per cent of which is Arabic in origin.

The Catholic influence accounts for the fact that there are no divorces in Malta, abortion is illegal, and local religious festivals erupt with colour and celebration.

Trade Links
Malta applied to join the Economic Union (EU) in 1990, but with the return to power of the Maltese Labour Party these plans have been withdrawn. Malta presently conducts three quarters of its trade with EU nations. There are also important trade links with Libya and North Africa.

Malta's first capital was the ancient town of Mdina, named by the Arabs who fortified it in the 9th century

7

Essence of Malta & Gozo

A village festival, like this one in Qrendi, is a social occasion as much as a religious one

Malta and Gozo draw together a richness of archaeological and architectural treasures, in an hospitable climate where the temperature climbs to 35°C and makes the clear sea the most excellent of baths, and water sports a pleasure. The islands come to life with festivals known as *festas* which open up Maltese culture to visitors. Even tourist enclaves have their own festivals every night in pubs and discos. The people are Malta's strongest asset. They are proud but not narrowly nationalistic, deeply religious but not repressive, courteous but not superficial. There is an enigma somewhere but it bothers no one.

THE 10 ESSENTIALS

If you only have a short time to visit Malta & Gozo, or would like to get a really complete picture of the country, here are the essentials:

• **See the *Malta Experience*** audio-visual show (➤ 110) in Valletta for an enjoyable dip into history, covering 7,000 years in 50 minutes.

• **Go to a *festa*,** the Maltese village festival, for the fun and vitality, the colour and the sound effects (➤ 116).

• **Enjoy Maltese food** by tucking into *pastizzi* (➤ 94) with your mid-morning drink, and have at least one picnic with fresh bread bought before 11AM and peppered cheese from Gozo.

• **Spend more than a day** in Gozo because the pleasure of being here lies in its unhurried pace and a quick visit will fail to do justice to its many charms (➤ 80 –91).

Civilization that 'the great temples of Malta and Gozo lay claim to be the world's most impressive prehistoric monuments' (➤ 16, and 26).

• **Go for a walk around Valletta,** visiting a church here, a museum or art gallery there, forts and gardens (➤ 33).

• **Buy some Maltese glass or Maltese lace** both artistic and affordable examples of Maltese handicrafts (➤ 105).

• **Visit St John's Co-Cathedral** in Valletta and see the Caravaggio paintings . The Italian painter came to Malta in 1607 and stayed only 14 months before he escaped from prison for an unknown crime (➤ 22).

• **See Mdina,** the ancient capital, walled by the Arabs and separated from the suburbs which became Rabat. History stares back at you from the walls (➤ 56).

• **Visit at least one of the prehistoric sites:** Ggantija, Tarxien, Għar Dalam. All bear testimony to Colin Renfrew's claim in *Before*

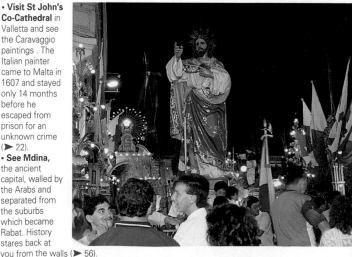

• **Take a cruise around the Grand Harbour** a magnificent and truly formidable sight that sparks the imagination (➤ 111).

Life-sized statues, carried on moveable frames feature in religious processions

9

The Shaping of Malta & Gozo

5500–4100 BC
The Neolithic Age, when Sicilian colonists live in cave dwellings or stone and wattle-and-daub huts, use decorated red and grey pottery and create clay figurines. They farm barley, wheat and lentils, keep domesticated animals and hunt using slingstones. They import obsidian and flint from Sicily to make knives. Skorba temples are built.

4100–2500 BC
The 'Copper Age', when the temples at Ġgantija, Tarxien and the Hypogeum at Ħal-Saflieni are built. This highly complex society has a priest class and a religion which includes a deity, oracles and animal sacrifice as well as intricate burial rites. Potters, architects and other craft workers make delicate woven cloth and highly decorated pots. Abruptly ends around 2500 BC.

2500–800 BC
The Bronze Age. This culture is in many ways inferior to that of the previous era. Information about the period comes from the Tarxien Cemetery. They cremate their dead and from the grave items left in funerary urns we

A 12th-century fresco from St Paul's and St Agatha's Catacombs

know that they weave cloth, use copper tools, and probably have links with other cultures in the Peloponnese peninsula and southern Italy. Only a few dolmen–type structures remain. Villages are fortified, and the mysterious cart ruts at Ghar il-Kibr appear.

c600 BC
Comes to be dominated by the Carthaginian trading empire. Phoenician colonists trade with Greece, build temples to the Phoenician gods, strike their own coins, and organise complex rock tomb burials. An inscription in both Greek and Phoenician helps decipher the Phoenician language.

257 BC
A Roman force invades during the Punic Wars (Romans against Carthaginians) and many settlements are totally devastated.

218 BC
Malta is incorporated into the Roman empire. Elaborate catacomb

burials become common. Punic temples are elaborated and Romanised villas appear in rural areas. Roman towns start to develop.

AD 58
St Paul, shipwrecked, converts the Roman governor to Christianity.

AD 500–870
Byzantine empire now in control.

AD 870–1090
Under Arab rule.

1090–1530
Colonised by succession of European powers: Normans, Germans, French and Spanish.

1429
Sacked by Muslims.

10

1530
Charles V of Spain gives islands in perpetuity to the Hospitallers Knights of the Order of St John of Jerusalem.

1565
The Great Siege. A Turkish fleet attacks the Order's settlement at Birgu, in the Grand Harbour, with the aim of taking Malta. After several months siege relief comes from allies in Sicily.

1566
The city of Valletta is founded.

1614
A second Turkish invasion is repelled.

1600s
A series of forts and

towers is built around the coast, but no further Turkish invasions occur.

1700s
Becomes a flourishing melting pot. The Order of St John of Jerusalem declines as a fighting force, turning to trade.

1798
Napoleon invades. The Knights are ejected, never to return. Wholesale looting of churches. The Maltese call on the British for their assistance.

1800
The French surrender and the British occupy the islands.

1814
The Treaty of Paris makes Malta a British Crown Colony.

1835–1932
Various attempts to establish a constitution fail.

1914–18
In World War I, becomes 'Nurse of the Mediterranean'.

1939
World War II makes Malta a strategic target, bringing great hardship.

A Maltese Knight in his armour stands to attention

1942
On 15 April, the people and the island of Malta are awarded the George Cross for gallantry, by King George VI. In April alone, over 6,000 tonnes of bombs fall.

1943
Italy and the Allies sign an armistice on board HMS *Nelson* in Grand Harbour.

1962
State of Malta is created.

1964
Malta achieves independence within the Commonwealth.

1971
The Labour Party, led by Dom Mintoff, elected.

1979
British forces withdraw.

1990
Malta applies for full membership of the EU.

1990
Pope John Paul II visits.

1992
HM Queen Elizabeth II visits for George Cross 50th anniversary celebrations.

1997
Labour Party returns to power.

Peace & Quiet

Birdwatching
With peace and quiet comes the pleasure of birdwatching. Seabirds, including shearwaters, may be spotted from the clifftops of Gozo and the Marfa Peninsula on Malta, and the islands' strategic position as a resting station has long been appreciated by migrant species passing between northern Europe and Africa. Some birds make Malta their winter home, but whatever the time of year a colourful birdlife may be observed.

Coming directly from the airport to the resorts of Buġibba or St Julian's one could be forgiven for thinking there is no peace and quiet in Malta. Fortunately – because of the islands of Gozo and Comino – it is easy to correct this fallacy.

Gozo's Appeal

Gozo may have one of the best discos and one of the best top class hotels in Malta (➤ 103), but the characteristic appeal of the place is not hedonistic. Given its small size one can cycle or walk anywhere along quiet country roads passing small family farms or following the rugged coastline along clifftop paths. Apart from the walk detailed later (➤ 87), other rewarding walks include Ta' Dbieġi Hill near the village of San Lawrenz, Hondoq ir-Rummien just south of Qala and San Blas Valley and Bay from Nadur.

The Blue Lagoon

The island of Comino (➤ 46) is inundated with boatloads of day visitors but it is the Blue Lagoon that is the focus of interest and, given the absence of cars and the small distances (hardly more than a kilometre in any direction), one may escape from people. It helps to be here in spring when flowers give joyful relief to the barren landscape. It is even better to stay the night, because after sunset or early in the morning you will have Comino to yourself.

Time and the tides have combined to form the beauty of the Blue Grotto

Parks and Gardens

On Malta itself there are numerous opportunities to escape the hustle and bustle. The tourist office has a useful brochure listing and describing the various parks and gardens where one can seek solace, shade and enjoy a picnic far away from the fast-food restaurants and the crowds. One of the most attractive and larger parks is the San Anton Gardens

(➤ 44) where some of the sub-tropical trees are labelled, including a splendid pair of wide-spreading Banyan trees, *Ficus benghalensis*, on the main path, and there is a small aviary to amuse young children.

Even the cacti blossom beautifully on the island of Gozo

Around Malta

Malta's capital city of Valletta is remarkably quiet and peaceful at night. Apart from a small number of restaurants and bars there is very little open after 7PM in the evening. A stroll up Triq Marsamxett to Fort St Elmo and back down the other side past the Lower Barracca Gardens is relaxing as well as offering fine views of Marsamxett Harbour and Grand Harbour (➤ 17).

The clifftop landscape in the southwest of Malta offers some of the best opportunities for getting away on one's own and, from April to June or September and October, this is a good place for bird watching. A recommended short walk is south from the village of Dingli (➤ 49) to the coast and then northwest along the ridge to Il-Qaws. With a good map one could thread one's way back to Rabat from here or return to Dingli for a bus.

> ### *Did you know ?*
>
> *The countryside often seems barren and sun-baked but suddenly between February and May it becomes surprisingly verdant, and crocuses, tulips and fritillarias shower the fields with colour.*
> *There are over 600 species of wildflowers. Gozo is always greener because of its clay soil and slightly hillier landscape.*

13

Famous of
Malta & Gozo

The Knights of Malta
The wealth of both the Order of St John and the Knights themselves attracted artists to the island with which the Order will be for ever associated. This ensured the presence of outstanding works of art and architecture, and formidable defences.
The Knights Hospitallers of the Order of St John of Jerusalem was a religious order founded in Jerusalem in the 11th century. After the capture of Jerusalem by the Muslims in 1187, the Order moved to Rhodes, but this, too, proved temporary.
In 1530 the emperor of the Holy Roman Empire gave them the Maltese islands. The Grand Master, Jean Parisot de la Valette, made it their permanent home and prevented Suleyman from conquering Malta in the Great Siege of 1565.
The order grouped the Knights according to language or country. Each of the eight *langues* had its own hostel or *auberge*, built around a courtyard. Five have survived. Originally hospitallers, the Knights had become warriors, then traders and indulged in baroque architecture. Rich living and dissoluteness led to their decline.

For such a small island, Malta's geographical position meant that it was destined to play a memorable role in world events, notably during the centuries under the Knights of Malta and in World War II.

Politics

Dom Mintoff (1916–), a controversial and charismatic figure, dominated Maltese, and sometimes British, politics for 30 years. From a poor family, he attended university in Malta and won a scholarship to Oxford. He joined the post-war, pro-British Labour Party of Malta. In 1955 he became Prime Minister, proposing the full integration of Malta into the United Kingdom, but Britain refused. Mintoff immediately changed his policy to one of full independence, and resigned in 1958 to lead the Malta Liberation Movement. It was the Nationalist Party that negotiated Malta's independence. Mintoff returned to power from 1971 to 1984. As a politician his chief concern was the welfare of Malta.

Art

Caravaggio (1571–1610), the greatest Italian painter of the 17th century, left his mark on the island after only a few months' stay here. He was notorious for his violent temper and, unusually, used common people as models for his paintings of the saints. Wanted for murder in Rome, he accepted a commission from the Order in 1607 and painted *The Beheading of St John the Baptist*. He became a Knight, completed three more paintings, but became involved in a fight and was expelled from the Order. He escaped from jail, and continued his short but colourful life elsewhere.

Among very many other famous artists over the centuries were the Spanish Mateo Perez d'Aleccio (1547–99), Italian Mattia Preti (1616–99), and the French Antoine de Favray (1706–98). Among the Maltese were sculptor Melchiorre Gafa (1635–67), Francesco Zahra (1710–73), Guiseppe Cali (1846–1930), and Antonio Sciortino (1879–1947).

Architecture

Lorenzo Gafa (1630–1710), brother of Melchiorre and famed for his domes, was one of many talented architects whose monuments still stand. Gerolamo Cassar (1520–86) designed a number of Valletta's buildings, including St John's Co-Cathedral, the Grand Master's Palace and all the *auberges*. His son Vittorio (d1605), with Grand Master Wignacourt, built Forts St Lucian and St Thomas. Others included Nadrea Beli (1705–72), Antonio Ferramolio (d1550) and Francesco Laparelli da Cortona (1521–70).

Top Ten

1
Ġgantija

✝ 83D3

✉ Ġantija, near Xagħra, Gozo

☎ 553194

🕐 1 Oct–31 Mar, Mon–Sat 08:30–4:30, Sun 8:30–3; 1 Apr–15 Jun, 8:30–6:30, Sun 8:30–3; 16 Jun–15 Sep, Mon–Sat 8:30–7, Sun 8:30–3; 16 Sep–30 Sep, Mon–Sat 8:30–6:30, Sun 8:30–3

🍴 Refreshment stalls (£) in the car park

🚌 64, 65 from Victoria

♿ Few

✋ Cheap

Even the temples at Ġgantija arouse curiosity

Immense bare rock, curious features and primitive attempts at decoration are the stunning signs of a 5,000-year-old technology and culture.

Dating back to 3500–3000 BC, Malta's 'Copper Age', the temples at Ġgantija on Gozo are thought to be the oldest free-standing monuments in the world. The site is an artificial plateau with a sweeping panorama. Primitive in structure, it is its size which creates a sense of wonder, particularly the outer walls. According to legend, they were built by a female giant. The coralline limestone blocks which make up the outer wall, some weighing as much as 20 tonnes, were quarried from the hill on the other side of the valley and probably rolled and dragged over using the rounded stones, that lie scattered around the front of the temples, as rollers. The blocks were stood upright by building earth ramps, and large vertical supporting slabs support smaller rectangular blocks.

The temples themselves tell us something about the organisation and religion of the complex society that built these structures. Two buildings, one larger and older than the other, seem to have been places of worship to a fertility goddess. It has even been suggested that the shape of the structures themselves represent the body of the goddess (head and breasts). Inside the smaller structure, about 200 years later in origin, stone female figures were found, although these belong to a later date than the construction of the buildings. In the doorway of the larger structure are hinge holes used to support doors which would once have separated the worshippers from the priests who were in the outer and central inner temples. Inside, two holes in the floor are thought to be libation holes where the blood of the sacrificed was poured. In the centre of the building, which was once 6m high with a domed roof, were found a large triangular stone and another one carved into the shape of a phallus.

2
Grand Harbour

*Spread out like a living painting,
several hundred years of history bake quietly in
the Mediterranean sunshine.*

The truly formidable ramparts are best viewed from one of the many boat trips which go out into the harbour for a day or half-day trip. However, if time does not allow for that there are several good viewing points from land, particularly from Upper Barracca Gardens (► 41). Boat tours generally leave from **Sliema Marina** passing Fort Manoel on the right and crossing Marsamxett Harbour where the northern fortifications of Valletta can be seen. Grand Harbour itself is guarded by the two forts of Fort St Elmo and Fort Ricasoli, appearing as the tour passes briefly into open sea before turning west into the harbour. As you pass Fort St Elmo damage done by the Italians in 1941 can still be seen.

 29E3

Sliema Marina

 Tours leave from Sliema Marina, check times

 Lunch and dinner cruises are available

 60, 61, 62, 63, 64, 67, 68 from Valletta, 70 from Buġibba, 65 from Rabat, 86 from Buġibba and Rabat, 645 from Cirkewwa, 652 from Golden Bay

 Valletta–Sliema ferry
(☎ 335689)

Built as a fortress city and developed as a naval base and dockyard by the British, Valletta sits snugly between this harbour and Marsamxett. Looking up at the towering eastern shore of Valletta the wharves of the marina with its 16th- and 17th-century buildings can be seen, surmounted by the Sacra Infermeria, Lower Barracca Gardens and Upper Barracca Gardens. Opposite Valletta's eastern defences are the fingers of land which make up Senglea and Vittoriosa. Between them can be seen the Cottonera Lines, a great 2-km inland defensive wall built in the 1670s. From the tips of these two points in 1565 the Knights of St John strung a chain to prevent the Turkish fleet of 200 vessels from entering Dockyard Creek, which was then the main harbour. Dominating the whole scene is Fort St Angelo (► 76).

The grandeur of fortress-like Valletta and the Grand Harbour, seen from the air .

3
Ħaġar Qim & Mnajdra

✝ 28C1

✉ 1.5km southwest of Qrendi

🕐 16 Jun–30 Sep: Mon–Sun 7:45–2. 1Oct–15 Jun: Mon–Sat 8:15–5, Sun 8:15–4:15

🍴 Bar and restaurant (££) near the car park

🚌 35

♿ Few

✋ Cheap

❓ Mnajdra is closed for some renovation work, so check.

Over a thousand years before the pyramids, two temples were built on an evocative and spectacular site close to the sea.

The two temple complexes illustrate the ingenuity and complex social structure of a society that lived here for 3,000 years, then suddenly disappeared between 2500 and 1800 BC. This is megalithic architecture of a high order.

Ħaġar Qim ('Standing Stones'), first excavated in 1839, is a series of radiating oval rooms added on at various times to a trefoil structure. Holes around the entrance show where hinged doors once stood with bars to lock them shut. The stone is soft globigerina limestone which was easy to decorate, as can be seen in the pitted and spiral decoration, which accordingly has weathered badly. One stone here measures 7m by 3m.

Mnajdra, the second temple site, is a five-minute walk away in the direction of the sea but in a more sheltered spot. Made from a harder coralline limestone, it is far better preserved. The three temples share a common outer wall and presumably at one time shared a roof. There are the same patterns of pitted and spiral decorations, an outer temple with inner sanctuaries, carved recesses, trilithion door frames (two large pillars holding up a third block) and, in the second temple, an oracular window (through which the high priest or oracle might have spoken).

Both Ħaġar Qim and Mnajdra are thought to be expressions of a fertility-worshipping religion. Carved obese female figures have been found at both sites, as well as

The megalithic architecture of Ħaġar Qim cannot fail to impress visitors

numerous other artefacts which can be seen in the Museum of Archaeology at Valletta (► 39).

The small islet to be seen out at sea is Filfa, just 1km in circumference.

4
Ħal-Saflieni Hypogeum

A vast and complex underground carved temple with catacombs is unique in Malta and in Europe.

This underground burial place and temple covering an area of 799sq m was discovered in 1902 by workmen, who were laying the foundations of a house when they broke through the roof of the upper temple. Realising that building would stop if the authorities discovered its existence, they kept quiet about it, but three years later the news was out. Eventually, the site was excavated and was discovered to consist of three levels of catacombs, descending to 11m, the highest and oldest level being naturally occurring chambers while the two lower levels were carved out of the soft limestone.

The top level was in use *c*3000 BC as a burial ground. Descending by modern stairs to the middle level the visitor encounters intricately carved pillars as well as spiral and hexagonal decorations, probably created around 2500 BC. This level has a chamber known as the 'Holy of Holies' with a carved façade of four pillars supporting a curved lintel and a vaulted roof. The Oracle Chamber, where part of the ceiling and walls are covered in red ochre, has 'supernatural' acoustics.

✚ 29E2

✉ Burials Street, Paola

☎ 825579

🕐 16 Jun–30 Sep:
Mon–Sun 7:45–2.
1 Oct –15 Jun: Mon–Sat
8:15–5 Sun 8:15–4:15

🍴 Cafés and restaurants in
Paola (£)

🚌 5, 11, 14

♿ None

✋ Cheap

❓ The Hypogeum has
been closed for
renovation since 1991,
but is due to open mid-
1997

The Ħal-Saflieni Hypogeum is one of the world's major archaeological sites

The lowest level is a maze of chambers carved supposedly as a burial place but never used, presumably because the event which wiped out this community around 2500 BC intervened.

It is thought that around 7,000 bodies were buried here during its later use. Besides the human remains, statues, amulets, vases and many other objects were found during excavation. Replicas of many of these can be seen at the small museum at the Hypogeum. The originals are in the Museum of Archaeology in Valletta. Since only 15 people can visit the Hypogeum at a time, a visit early in the day is recommended before the queues form.

5
National Museum of Fine Arts

✚ 34C4

✉ South Street, Valletta

☎ 225769

🕐 1 Oct–15 Jun: Mon–Sat 8:15–5; Sun 8:15–4:15. 16 Jun–30 Sep: Mon–Sun 7:45– 2

🍴 The Scalini restaurant (£) opposite (➤ 93) or the Union Cafeteria (£) a few metres down in the Workers' Memorial Building

♿ None

💷 Cheap

On entering the welcome cool and elegant interior of the building one finds oneself in a treasure house of Western European art.

This notable building dates back to the 16th century when it was the palace of a French Knight. Famous figures inhabiting it over the centuries included Charles d'Orleans, brother of King Louis Philippe of France, who died here. For a time it was the British Admiralty House until returning to Maltese ownership in 1961; it became the home of the museum in 1974. The whole style of the building, including the magnificent staircase with two flights of semicircular steps, contributes a sense of serenity and elegance to what is a major collection of art. On three floors there are 30 rooms full of remarkable paintings. On the first floor, over a dozen rooms display paintings from the 14th to 17th centuries representing Venetian, Dutch and Italian schools. Plaster models by the local artist Sciortino are also here. Mattia Preti is well represented in rooms 12 and 13 with works such as *The Martyrdom of St Catherine*, while room 14 has paintings by Antoine de Favray and is known as Favray's Room. In rooms 4 and 6 are paintings by Domenico Tintoretto (a relative of the famous Tintoretto), Palma il Giovane and Andrea Vincentino.

Rooms 20 to 24 are dedicated to Maltese artists. In room 24 exhibitions of modern works by Maltese artists are changed regularly.

Worth a visit on its own, in the basement is a display of relics from the period of the Knights, ranging from medical equipment to church silver and various religious artefacts.

Visit to a Maltese House *by Antoine de Favray*

6
Palace of the Grand Masters

The official residence of the Grand Masters until 1798 is now home to Malta's Parliament.

The Palace was originally a great house built for a Grand Master's nephew in 1569. It was extended two years later by Gerolamo Cassar into a two-storey building enclosing two courtyards: Neptune Court, with its central bronze statue of Neptune, and Prince Alfred Court, each entered by a separate doorway in the rather plain façade. In Prince Alfred's Court note the Pinto Clock tower with its mechanical figures, erected in 1745.

Inside, many of the State apartments are decorated with friezes depicting episodes from the history of the Order. There are portraits of the Grand Masters and of European monarchs, interesting furniture and works of art. In the Small Council Chamber are particularly beautiful 18th-century Gobelin tapestries. In the Hall of St Michael and St George, once the throne room, are paintings, notably a frieze showing the Great Siege by Mateo Perez d'Aleccio, a pupil of Michaelangelo. The Hall of Ambassadors is hung with red damask, paintings and another d'Aleccio frieze. The Yellow State Room, once the room where the Grand Master's retinue of pages lived, has paintings by Batoni and Ribera.

Prince Albert's Court leads to the Armoury, a converted stables, which for those with children will be the most interesting part of the visit. Here hundreds of exhibits of armour, weaponry and ordnance date back to the siege of 1565. Looking at the armour you understand why the circular steps leading up to the main building are so shallow: one suit weighed as much as 50kg, making it difficult for a knight in full armour to climb them.

🚩 35D4

✉ Palace Square, Republic Street, Valletta

☎ 221221

🕐 1 Oct–15 Jun:
Mon–Wed 0:30 3:45,
Thu–Fri 8:30–4.
16Jun–30 Sep: Mon–Fri 8–12:45.

🍴 Bologna Restaurant (££) nearby (➤ 92)

♿ Few

✋ Cheap

❓ The Palace is closed to visitors when Parliament is sitting

An army in waiting at the Palace of the Grand Masters in Valletta

7
St John's Co-Cathedral & Museum

Its austere, 16th-century exterior belies the stunning baroque interior, where the magnificence and wealth of the Order burgeons in works of art.

Prepare to be astonished when first entering St John's Co-Cathedral

Built in the 16th century to a simple Mannerist design by Gerolamo Cassar, this was until 1798 the Conventual Church of the Order of the Knights of St John. The wide plain façade with two bell towers of the Co-Cathedral ('Co-' because there are two cathedrals) seems dull. Once inside though, there is almost too much to take in. It is outstanding on several levels: its historical associations, the proportions of its architecture, its rich decoration and the great diversity of its treasures. On promotion, every Knight was required to make a gift to the Order's church.

The interior, once as austere as its exterior, was redesigned in the baroque style under the supervision of Mattia Preti. A central nave has side chapels each dedicated to a different *langue* of the order. On the barrel-vaulted ceiling is a series of oil on plaster paintings by Preti showing 18 episodes in the life of St John the Baptist. The striking floor is paved with the ornate and highly individual multi-coloured marble tombstones of Knights.

At the left of the main door is the Chapel of Germany, dedicated to the Epiphany. The altarpiece is 17th century by Erardi. Through the narrow ambulatory is the Chapel of Italy which once held Caravaggio's painting *St Jerome* (now in the cathedral museum). Next, the Chapel of France, restored in the 1840s during a brief period of revulsion against baroque, has an altarpiece by Preti. The Chapel of Provence has a painting of St Michael above the altar. Beyond it is the Chapel of the Holy Relics, looted by Napoleon in 1798. Above the crypt, (usually closed to the public) is the marble, lapis lazuli and bronze altar. The huge marble group in the apse by Giuseppe Mazzuoli depicts the baptism of Christ.

Across the nave is the Chapel of the Blessed Sacrament. Legend says that its silver gates were painted black to make them appear worthless during the looting by Napoleon. Inside is an icon, the *Madonna of Carafa*, presented to the order in 1617 by a Knight.

The Chapel of Auvergne has three works by Giuseppe d'Arena, while the Chapel of Aragon contains the first piece of work done by Preti for the Knights, *St George and*

✝ 34D3

✉ St John's Square, Valletta

☎ 220536

🕐 Mon–Fri 9:30–12:30, 1:30–4:30, Sat 9:30–12:30. Closed public holidays.

🍴 Café Marquee (£) is opposite (► 92)

♿ None

✋ Cheap

❓ Sunday High Mass at 9:15 AM in Latin and masses in the vernacular on church festivities and days of commemoration.

the Dragon. Painted in 1658 in Naples it was his sample of work aimed at obtaining the commission for the vault. Going beyond the entrance to the Oratory the last chapel is that of Castile et Léon, dedicated to St James and containing Preti's last work. Preti himself was made a Knight and his tombstone is in the sacristy.

The oratory and museum contain more wonders, including two Caravaggio paintings, *St Jerome* and *The Beheading of St John the Baptist*, the latter considered to be his finest. Also on display are antiphonaries (books of chants), the surviving cathedral silver, and the Flemish tapestries depicting religious stories made in the late 17th century at a huge cost. The tapestries decorate the nave during the *festa* of St John.

The rather austere exterior of St John's Co-Cathedral, built between 1573 and 1577

23

8

St Paul's & St Agatha's Catacombs

✝ 56A1/B1

✉ Triq Sant'Agata, Rabat

☎ 454562 (St Paul's);
454503 (St Agatha's)

🕐 Mon–Fri 9–12, 1–4, Sat
9–1. Closed Sundays
and public holidays

🍴 Cafés and restaurants
(£) nearby

🚌 80, 81, 83, 84, 86 from
Valletta, 65 from Sliema

♿ None

✊ Cheap

↔ St Paul's Church and
Grotto (➤ 59),
St Augustine's Church
(➤ 59)

*The crypt where
St Agatha is said to have
prayed while on the island
in AD250. The frescoes
are late 15th century, the
altar is late 17th century*

*Wander among 3sq km of dimly lit, claustrophobic,
and eerily empty tombs
under Rabat.*

St Paul's Catacombs, the largest of Rabat's catacomb complexes, is a labyrinth of corridors and burial chambers. Although plundered many years ago, the empty graves are in three basic styles. The canopied grave is a little like a four-poster bed, with a flat slab overhung with a canopy cut out of the soft limestone rock. Another type is the saddest: the *loculus*, a tiny rectangular recess cut into the wall to hold the grave of a child. Others called floor graves are cut into the floor and would have been covered with a slab of rock. A thousand corpses must once have rested here. Scattered around the graves are roughly hewn tables with circular benches around them. They were probably used by the families of the recently entombed for a religious service after the burial, or on anniversaries.

Close by, St Agatha's catacombs, below the church, are so named because the saint is said to have lived here for a while to escape the attentions of the Emperor Dedius. Fewer catacombs are visited on the 30-minute tour, but there are over 30 frescoes dating back to the 12th to 15th centuries, depicting St Agatha and other Christian figures. Here is the *arcosolium* type of tomb: arched windows cut into the rock wall. In the convent beside St Agatha's Church is a museum with related and unrelated exhibits, and outside is a good green area where you can rest to recover from the gloom and low ceilings.

9

St Paul's Cathedral

*An ancient cathedral which is a masterpiece
in itself as well as a treasure chamber of
Maltese baroque art.*

The belfries and dome – probably the finest on Malta –
dominate the skyline, and the frontal exterior with three
balanced bays separated by Corinthian pillars has an
altogether grander presence than that of St John's Co-
Cathedral in Valletta. This is the finest of Lorenzo Gafà's
churches, built between 1697 and 1702. However, the
interior, in the form of a Latin cross, may seem gloomy
despite the profusion of reds and golds. There are
numerous frescoes by Preti showing events in the life of
St Paul, including the saint's appearance on a white horse
when the city was besieged by Saracens in 1442. The
vaulted ceiling is covered in more frescoes by Vincenzo
and Antonio Manno. The carved Irish bog-oak doors to the
sacristy were part of the original church which was
destroyed in the earthquake of 1693. The floor is covered
in the funerary slabs of church and local dignitaries. In the
Chapel of the Blessed Sacrament is a 12th-century icon of
the Madonna and Child. The marble font is 15th century,
while the marquetry stalls date from 1481.

✚ 59C3

✉ St Paul's Square, Mdina

☎ 454136 (cathedral);
456497 (museum)

🕐 Mon–Sat 9–1,
1:30–4:30. Sun open
only for Mass. Museum
Mon–Sat 9–1,
1:30–4:30

🍴 Cafés and restaurants
(£–££) nearby (➤ 95–6)

🚌 80, 81, 83, 84, 86 from
Valletta, 65 from Sliema

♿ None

✋ Cheap

↔ Mdina and Rabat
(➤ 56–60)

❓ Festival of Conversion of
St Paul, 25 Jan. Festival
of St Peter and St Paul,
29 Jun. Pontifical
masses on Church
festivals. No admittance
to non-devotees during
church services

*The baroque beauty of
the magnificent St Paul's
Cathedral*

The museum stands on an ancient site, thought to be
the villa of Publius the Roman governor who was
converted to Christianity by St Paul. The collection of
artwork donated in 1833 includes works by Dürer and
Goya, while later donations include *St John the Baptist* by
Ferretti and *The Adoration of the Shepherds* by Subleyras.
There are vestments of ancient lace, manuscripts, and
collections of silver and coins. The ground floor has a
collection of Punic and Roman items, while the corridor
contains the original panels from the 14th-century choir
stalls of the cathedral.

10
Tarxien Temples

✝ 29E2

✉ Neolithic Temples Street, Tarxien

☎ 695578

🕐 1 Oct–15 Jun: Mon–Sat 8:30–4:30; Sun 8:30–3. 16 Jun–30 Sep: Mon–Sun 7:45–1:30

🍴 Nearest place for food in the main square in Paola, a seven-minute walk away (£)

🚌 11, 26

♿ Good

💷 Cheap

↔ Ħal-Saflieni Hypogeum (► 19)

The largest of the prehistoric remains was a rich depository of art, created by temple builders, and in striking contrast to the nearby Hypogeum.

The oldest of the three temples in this complex is some 6,000 years old, while the other two temples were built at later stages, presumably as additions to the original. The South Temple, the first temple you come to, was the second to have been built. It has a central paved square surrounded by carved stone benches and a ritual fire was probably lit in the centre of this area. There is a stone basin and an altar, both used in the ceremonies that took place. Many remains were found here, including burnt bones of animals, which are represented on the frieze around the next chamber's walls. The most imposing of the buildings, the Central Temple, was the last to be built (c2400 BC) at the peak of the Taxien period. It too has a central paved area with a hearth for sacrificial fires. One of the side rooms contains a huge bowl carved out of a single piece of stone. These rooms were probably secret areas open only to the priesthood. Most of these temples' doorways show bar holes where doors or screens would have been fitted. The third and oldest of the temples, the East Temple, has a similar structure, although it must have been altered to accommodate the middle building. It has the remains of a small chamber built into the walls with a tiny hole from which perhaps an oracle spoke. Outside are the stone balls used to roll the huge slabs of stone into place, while behind the temple complex are the ruins of an even earlier building with a possible hypogeum beneath it. To the right of the entrance gate is a stone block with cone-shaped indentations. The small stone balls found nearby suggest some kind of divination machine which predicted the future according to the movement of the balls. Visit the National Museum of Archaeology in Valletta (► 39) to see finds from the site and an artist's impression of what the temples once looked like.

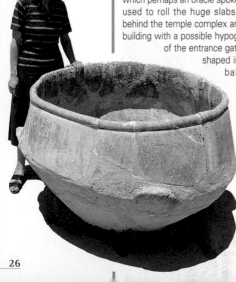

Artefacts at the Tarxien Temples point to ancient rituals from the prehistoric past

What To See

Orejten Point

Bahar iċ-Ċaghaq

Ras L-Irqieqa

Madliena Fort
Gharghur

St Andrew's

Dragonara Point

St Julian's
St Julian's Bay

Sliema

San Gwann

Gżira

Balzan

Dragutt Point

Birkirkara

Ta'Xbiex

Marsamxett Harbour

VALLETTA

Fort Ricasoli

Wignacourt Aqueduct

Msida

Floriana

Fort St Roco
(Mediterranean Film Studios)

Santa Venera

Casa Leoni

Grand Harbour

Vittoriosa

Kalkara

Hamrun

Wied Is-Sewda

Qormi

Senglea

Cospicua

Xghajra

Marsa Sports Club

Marsa

Paola

Żabbar

Wied Hanzir

Wied il-Kbir

Hompesch Arch

Tarxien Temples

Museum of Religious Art

Hypogeum

Żonqor Point

Marsaskala Bay

Luqa

Tarxien

Marsaskala

St Thomas Tower

Il-Gżira

Żejtun

Mamo Tower

St Thomas Bay

Luqa Airport

Misrah Strejnu

Gudja

Mqabba

Ghaxaq

Marsaxlokk

Tal-Mentna Catacombs

Kirkop

Tas Silġ

Hofra l-Kbria

Gwarena Tower

Ħal Millieri

Safi

Ghar Dalam Cave & Museum

Marsaxlokk

St Lucian Tower

Hofra l'z-Żghira

Qrendi

Żurrieq

Borġ in-Nadur

Peter's Pool

Il Maqluba

Birżebbuġa

Nigret

Bubaqra

Pinto Battery
Gorbachev/
Bush Monument

St George's Bay

Pretty Bay

Fort Delimara

Wied iż-Żurrieq

Marsaxlokk Bay

Delimara Point

Blue Grotto

Kalafrana

Malta Freeport

Fort Benghisa

Ghar Hasan Cave

Benghisa Point

D   E   F

Valletta

All roads lead to Valletta. Nearly every bus route on the island starts and ends in the capital and anyone visiting Malta for the first time will spend some time here. The city was built after the Great Siege to create an impregnable fortress against another assault. It retains the feel of a fortified city, but is much more than a defensive town. Valletta was built as a home for the aristocratic Order of the Knights of St John, which ensured exemplary architecture, in a culturally rich Renaissance city. Despite intensive bombing during World War II, the city remains intact and visually imposing. The streets were built on a simple grid-plan but rocky terrain meant few level surfaces. The constantly shifting levels bring to mind Byron's 'cursed streets of stairs'.

---

*'Adieu, ye joys of
La Valette!
Adieu, sirocco, sun and
sweat!
Adieu, thou palace rarely
enter'd!
Adieu, ye mansions where –
I've ventured!
Adieu, ye cursed streets of
stairs!'*

LORD BYRON
Farewell to Malta (1811)

Valletta

Francesco Laparelli da Cortona, a military engineer, arrived in Malta in 1565. His brief was to help plan a city that would permanently minimise the Turkish threat. A rocky peninsula in the north of the island was chosen as the site for a completely new city and what you see today is largely unchanged from what Laparelli planned and what his Maltese assistant, Geralamo Cassar, filled with extraordinary architecture. Valletta was the first planned city in Europe.

Everyone enters Valletta through the City Gate and passes directly into the pedestrianised Republic Street. It is the spine of the city that runs in a straight line for 1.5 km to Fort St Elmo at the northeast tip of the peninsula. The street passes across a number of squares, each rich in history and architecture, with bisecting side streets that lead down to one of the two enclosing harbours. Driving into Valletta is pointless because of its small size and 'streets of stairs', but this makes it ideal for walking. The city changes character during the course of the day, the best time to visit being the morning when shops, restaurants, churches and museums are open and there is a buzz to this tiny metropolis. The afternoons are suitable for slow walks, but the streets are then devoid of people and most places are closed for an enviably long siesta. Early evening is a little more animated, especially at weekends, but the nights are strangely quiet as Valletta retreats into itself.

Byron's 'cursed streets of stairs' are trodden by few during the afternoon hours

31

What to See in Valletta

AUBERGE DE CASTILE ET LÉON

The Auberge de Castile is strategically located close to the ramparts and it is the city's most impressive example of *auberge* architecture. It dates from 1574 but the imposing baroque façade was added in the mid-18th century under Grand Master Pinto, a flamboyant bust of whom decorates the top of the stately doorway. Another admirable feature is the cornice that frames the building's roof and blends harmoniously with the louvred windows. The overall effect is that of baroque architecture at its most graceful and least complicated. The British Army had its headquarters here, and today it houses the prime minister's office.

BIBLIOTHECA (NATIONAL LIBRARY)

This grand, late 18th-century, Venetian-style building was the last public building commissioned by the Knights. It now houses some 400,000 works, many rare or priceless, and a small selection is on display in the main hall, including the 12th-century Papal Bull instituting the Order of Knights and the 1530 Deed of Donation of Malta to the Order by Charles V. The walls of the hall are lined with books in their fine bindings. All archival material covering the history of the Knights from 1113 to 1798 is lodged in the library and it is an important source of research material for historians.

CASA ROCCA PICCOLA

This late 16th-century dwelling was built for the Italian Knight Pietro La Rocca and is worth visiting for its period antiques. The bedroom contains a beautiful four-poster bed, the library has an intriguing wall-cabinet that functioned as a portable chapel and the various other rooms have a fascinating variety of antiques and paintings.

> ### Did you know ?
> The Order adopted the distinctive Maltese Cross in the mid-13th century. Each of the eight points symbolises one of the eight beatitudes, given in Christ's sermon on the Mount. The points also represent the eight langues of the Order. The four main sections represent the virtues of Fortitude, Justice, Temperance and Prudence, while white denotes purity.

35D3
Castile Square.
Not open to the public
Cafés and restaurants (£–££) within walking distance
Good
Upper Barracca Gardens (➤ 41)

35D3
Republic Square
224338
16 Jun–30 Sep: Mon–Sat 8:15–1:15PM. 1 Oct–15 Jun: Mon–Fri 8:15–5:45; Sat 8:15–1:15PM
Cafés and restaurants (£–££) in Republic Square
None
Free
Republic Square (➤ 40)

35E4
74 Republic Street
231796
Mon–Sat 10–1PM
Cafés and restaurants (£–££) within walking distance
Chair-bound visitors can be helped up the stairs and the doors on the first floor are wide enough to accommodate wheel chairs
Moderate
Palace of the Grand Masters (➤ 21), The Wartime Experience (➤ 41)
Guided tours on the hour

A Valletta Walk

This walk begins past the Triton Fountain and through the City Gate, once the main entrance into the citadel.

Take the first right into Ordnance St, passing the Post Office parcel department, but staying on the other side of the road to pass La Vittoria (➤ 38) and go into Castile Square.

The Auberge de Castile et Léon (➤ 32) is on the corner with Triq'il Merkanti (Merchants Street). Here is a bustling scene where bargains can be found and there is a morning market.

Walk down Merchants Street, past the Castellania.

The building opposite the post office, austere 18th-century Palazzo Parisio, is where Napoleon stayed *en route* to Egypt in 1798.

The next left allows for a detour to St John's Co-Cathedral (➤ 22–23) but return to Merchants Street for a right turn into Triq Santa Lucia (St Lucia Street) and the Church of St Paul's Shipwreck (➤ 41). Return to the Merchants Street junction but cross straight over, and turn right into Republic Street and Republic Square (➤ 40).

It may be time for an alfresco drink or meal in the tree-lined square.

Continue the walk by turning left into Triq'il Teatru (Old Theatre Street), crossing three junctions and passing the delightful Manoel Theatre (➤ 39) before turning right into West Street. Continue down this street until reaching the seawall where a right turn brings Fort St Elmo into view.

Head for the fort alongside the massive city walls overlooking St Elmo Bay taking time to contemplate the awesome defences. This walk ends at Fort St Elmo (➤ 38) at the point.

Distance
2km

Time
2-4 hours, depending on visits

Start point
City Gate
⊞ 34C3

End point
Fort St Elmo
⊞ 35F5

🛈 Tourist Information,
1 City Gate (☎ 237747)

Lunch
Eddie's (£)
✉ Republic Square
☎ 246454

The Italianate style of the Auberge de Castile et Léon

VALLETTA

Fort Manoel

Manoel Island

Royal Malta Yacht Club

5

Harbour

Marsamxett

Water Polo Pitch

Manderaggio

St Salvatore Bastion

St Andrew's Bastion

PJAZZA MATTIA PRETI

4

St Michael's Bastion

National Museum of Fine Arts

TRIQ NOFS IN NHAR

TRIQ BRITANJA

TRIQ IŻ LTEHAN

Embassy of the Order of St John

Museum of Archeology

Church of Santa Barbara

Hastings Gardens

St John's Cavalier

St Catherine's Church

City Gate

Ruins of the Royal Opera House

3

BELTISSEBH

TRIQ L-ASSEDJU L-KBIR

Triton Fountain

TRIQ IR-REPUBBLIKA

La Vittoria (Church of Our Lady of Victories)

City Gate Bus Terminus

St James' Cavalier

Independence Arena

St James' Bastion

FLORIANA

RAF Memorial

TRIQ NELSON

TRIQ ID-DUKA TA' YORK

2

PJAZZA SAN KALCIDONJU

TRIQ BRITANJA

IL-MALL

Maglio Gardens

TRIQ SARRIA

St Paul Boffa Hospital

Argotti Botanical Gardens

St Publius Church

TRIQ SANT' ANNA

TRIQ PINTO

1

Sarria Chapel

Crucifix Bastion

Porte des Bombes

A

B

C

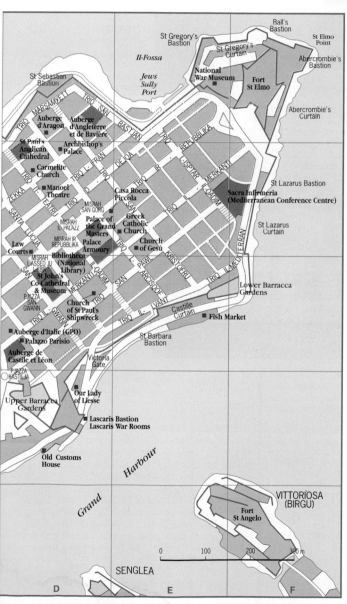

Ball's Bastion

St Gregory's Bastion

St Gregory's Curtain

St Elmo Point

Abercrombie's Bastion

Il-Fossa

Jews Sully Port

National War Museum

Fort St Elmo

St Sebastian Bastion

Abercrombie's Curtain

Auberge d'Aragon

Auberge d'Angleterre et de Bavière

Archbishop's Palace

St Paul's Anglican Cathedral

Carmelite Church

Manoel Theatre

Casa Rocca Piccola

St Lazarus Bastion

Sacra Infirmeria (Mediterranean Conference Centre)

MISRAH SAN GORG

Palace of the Grand Masters

Greek Catholic Church

St Lazarus Curtain

MISRAH IL-PALAZZ

MISRAH IR-REPUBBLIKA

Palace Armoury

Church of Gesù

Law Courts

Bibliotheca (National Library)

MISRAH SAN GWANN

MISRAH CLASSED JU

St John's Co-Cathedral & Museum

PJAZZA SAN GWANN

Church of St Paul's Shipwreck

Lower Barracca Gardens

Auberge d'Italie (GPO)

Palazzo Parisio

Castille Curtain

Fish Market

St Barbara Bastion

Auberge de Castille et Léon

PJAZZA KASTILJA

Victoria Gate

Upper Barracca Gardens

Our Lady of Liesse

Lascaris Bastion
Lascaris War Rooms

Old Customs House

Harbour

VITTORÍOSA (BIRGU)

Fort St Angelo

Grand

0   100   200   300 m

SENGLEA

D   E   F

FLORIANA ⬤⬤

This pleasant suburb of Valletta is best explored on foot (➤ 37) and although it was largely rebuilt after World War II there are some notable reminders of the past. Paolo Floriani was an Italian military engineer sent by the Pope in 1634 to further strengthen Valletta by a secondary defence system (Floriana Lines) outside the city.

The largest structure is **St Publius Church** which was finally completed in 1792, nearly 40 years after the first stone was laid, while its classical portico is a late 19th-century addition. The entire edifice was largely rebuilt after extensive damage during World War II. The vast open space in front of the church is distinguished by a number of large stone caps which are the protruding lids to over 70 granary pits. The pits were dug in the 17th century to store food safely and they were used again from 1941 to 1943 when Malta was once more under siege.

One of the most singular churches in Malta is the circular and compact Sarria Church, built in 1676 to fulfill a vow that was made by the Order of St John at the height of a terrible plague earlier in the year. Opposite the church is the Wignacourt Water Tower, an elaborate fountain that was constructed under Grand Master Wignacourt in 1615, part of an aqueduct system built to supply Valletta with water from the hills around Mdina. The nearby Argotti Botanical Gardens, with exotic trees and rare cacti, offer an escape from the traffic that pours through Floriana. So too does Maglio Gardens, a cultured strip of garden and tree-lined walkway that stretches from the Argotti Gardens back towards Valletta.

Above: The Grand Masters often built on a grand scale but Wagnacourt Tower is a more modest edifice

➕ 34B2

✉ To the immediate south of Valletta, a few minutes walk from the city's bus terminal

🕐 St Publius Church is open for services on Saturday evening and Sunday morning. Sarria Church has a Sunday morning service at 10:30

🍴 Cafés and restaurants (£–££) within walking distance in Valletta

♿ Good

🚌 Valletta (➤ 31)

A Walk in Floriana

To see Floriana and have an interesting, pleasing stroll, begin at the Phoenicia Hotel.

With your back to the Phoenicia Hotel's entrance, turn right and walk down to the Independence Monument in the middle of the road. The entrance to the Maglio Gardens is immediately behind the statue. Enter the park, designed by a Grand Master as a place for young knights to exercise by playing a ball game in a large, narrow structure, since demolished. The shaded pathway is dotted with busts of various Maltese dignitaries. Over to the left can be clearly seen the notable flat caps of the subterranean granary silos in the huge square in front of St Publius Church (➤ 36).

At the end of the park's walkway exit on the left side to view the Wignacourt Water Tower and Sarria Church on the other side of the road (➤ 36). Enter Argotti Botanical Gardens by the side of the water tower. The gardens, dating back to the late 18th century, are well-maintained and there are a number of cacti and exotic trees to admire. At the end of the walkway there is a good view from the balcony of the suburbs stretching across to Marsamxett Harbour.

Retrace your steps to the park's entrance and cross the road to the Sarria Church. Follow the road down to the right until it meets the main road at a junction with a statue of a decrepit-looking lion gracing a fountain. Turn left and walk up the main road towards Valletta, past shops and the American Consular office, to a roundabout. Keep to the left and the Phoenicia Hotel will be seen again on the other side of the car park.

Distance
2km

Time
1 hour

Start point
Phoenicia Hotel
➕ 34B2

End point
Phoenicia Hotel
➕ 34B2

Lunch
Phoenicia Hotel (£££)
✉ The Mall
☎ 225241

Part of the collection of cacti and succulent plants at the Argotti Botanical Gardens

37

Right: *Before restoration the Manoel Theatre first served as a hostel for the homeless: later it functioned as a cinema*

FORT ST ELMO

The vulnerable tip of the Valletta peninsula was chosen by the Order of St John as the best site for their fortifications, and the fort they built was sorely tested 13 years later in 1565 when the Turks laid siege. The fort withstood the attack for 31 days. The Knights were eventually forced to surrender, but the Turks' pyrrhic victory – their losses were more than four times those of the Christians – only served to endorse the value of St Elmo, and so the fort was rebuilt and enlarged. Its star-shaped design allowed for watch towers to be strategically angled so as to guard the entrances to both harbours and the British added gun emplacements in the 19th and 20th centuries. The Wartime Experience film (➤ 41) includes an account of a daring E-boat raid by the Italians in 1941 that was defeated by the guns of St Elmo. The fort, used in the making of the film *Midnight Express*, is open to the public and it is well worth seeing.

LA VITTORIA
(CHURCH OF OUR LADY OF VICTORIES)

This church's appearance belies its historical significance,

being Valletta's first place of worship when it was built in 1567 to commemorate the end of the siege, and now the oldest building in Valletta. Underneath the altar is the first stone laid in the building of Valletta, placed there by Grand Master La Valette. The present baroque façade and the bust of Pope Innocent XI were added in the late 17th century. Near by is a statue of Sir Paul Boffa, a former Prime Minister of Malta.

THE LASCARIS WAR ROOMS

The War Rooms were named after a French knight Jean Lascaris who became Grand Master (1636–57). The rooms were dug into the rock beneath Lascaris Bastion, and formed the subterranean headquarters of the island's defence system during the punishing bombardment of World War II, when Malta was an exceptionally heavily bombed target. Interesting displays, diagrams, photographs and dioramas complement the carefully refurbished command rooms.

Sidebar (Fort St Elmo):

✛ 35F5
✉ End of Republic Street and Merchants Street
🕐 Sat 1–5, Sun 9–5
🍴 Café (£) near by at the Sacra Infermeria/Malta Experience
♿ None
💷 Cheap
↔ National War Museum (➤ 40), Sacra Infermeria and Malta Experience (➤ 40 and 110)
❓ At 11AM and 8PM, in the summer, there are historical parades at the fort.

Sidebar (La Vittoria):

✛ 34C2
✉ Ordnance St
🍴 Cafés and restaurants (£) within walking distance
♿ Few
↔ Auberge de Castile et Léon (➤ 32)

Grand Master Ramon Perellos donated the pope's bust as a way of saying thank you to the Pope for ending a dispute with the Bishop

Sidebar (The Lascaris War Rooms):

✛ 35D2
✉ Upper Barracca Gardens
☎ 234936
🕐 Mon–Fri 9:30–4,Sat–Sun 9:30–12:30
🍴 Cafés and restaurants (£–££), walking distance
♿ None
💷 Cheap

MANOEL THEATRE ✪✪

The Knights so much enjoyed dramatic performances in their *auberges*, that in 1731 they commissioned the building of their own theatre. This opened the following year with the opera *Merope* by Maffei. After a long period of disuse, then conversion to a hostel for the homeless and later a cinema, this gem of a theatre was beautifully restored in 1960. The stalls area is tiny, as is the stage, but enclosing both are three tiers of ornately decorated boxes in soft green and gold and above them a gallery area from where a spectator could reach out and touch the gilded ceiling which has a solitary chandelier in its centre. If there is an opportunity to see any performance do not hesitate to book.

MUSEUM OF ARCHAEOLOGY ✪✪✪

The Museum of Archaeology building was once the Auberge de Provence, built in 1575 and home to the most prestigious group of Knights. Although it has undergone considerable modification over the centuries, it still has its main hall where the Knights dined on iced dishes (remarkably, the ice came from Sicily). The building now houses an important collection of antiquities, and a visit is recommended as a preliminary to seeing the major prehistoric sites in Malta and Gozo. There are important sculptures from the Tarxien Temples (➤ 26), including the bulbous lower half of a fertility goddess that would have stood over 2m high. From Ħaġar Qim (➤ 18) there is a superb limestone altar and there are a number of Roman antiquities, including a huge anchor that was discovered off the northern coast in the 1960s.

✚ 35D4
✉ Triq it-Teatru il-Qadim (Old Theatre Street)
☎ 222618
⏲ Guided tours: Mon–Fri 10:45 and 11:30, Sat 11:30. Theatre season Oct–May
🍴 Café (£)
♿ None **💶** Cheap
↔ Palace of the Grand Masters (➤ 21), Bibliotheca (➤ 32), Republic Square (➤ 40)

✚ 34C3
✉ Republic Street
☎ 221623
⏲ Summer daily 7:45–2. Winter Mon–Sat 8:15–5; Sun 8:15–4:15
🍴 Cafés and restaurants (£) within walking distance
❓ Temporarily closed due to renovation and redecoration; expected to reopen in 1997

NATIONAL MUSEUM OF FINE ARTS (➤ 20, TOP TEN)

NATIONAL WAR MUSEUM ✪✪

Located under the ramparts facing Marsamxett Harbour, the vaulted hall of the War Museum is packed with

hardware, photographs and memorabilia from World War II. One of the most famous exhibits is the wingless Gladiator biplane, *Faith*, the sole survivor of the *Faith*, *Hope* and *Charity* trio of planes that formed Malta's aerial defence in 1940. Also on display is the George Cross that the people of Malta received for their heroism in 1942.

PALACE OF THE GRAND MASTERS (➤ 21, TOP TEN)

REPUBLIC SQUARE ✪✪

The surrounding cafés and their outdoor tables have made this centrally located square a natural meeting place and point of orientation in Valletta. It was called Queen's Square under the British who reinforced the point by placing a statue of Queen Victoria here in 1891. The lace-clad queen now surveys the tourists who enjoy watching the world go by under the superb backdrop of the Bibliotheca.

SACRA INFERMERIA ✪✪

The Order of St John may have degenerated into an aristocrat's club but it began life as an association of noble hospitallers, so not surprisingly the Holy Infirmary (Sacra Infermeria) was one of Valletta's early buildings, receiving its first patients in 1574. It soon became famous for its high standards, as well as its grand interior. The Great Ward, 153m long, has one of the longest unsupported roof expanses in Europe. During World War II it was seriously damaged through bombing and after extensive renovation it reopened as the Mediterranean Conference Centre. See the excellent Malta Experience (➤ 110) audio-visual film show here in a modern auditorium.

ST JOHN'S CO-CATHEDRAL AND MUSEUM
(➤ 22–3, TOP TEN)

✚ 35E5
✉ Lower St Elmo on French Curtain
☎ 222430
🕐 16 Jun–30 Sep: Mon–Sat 7:45–2PM. 1 Oct–15 Jun: Mon–Sat 8:15–5,Sun 8:15–4:15
🍴 Nearest café (£) is at the Sacra Infermeria
♿ Few
✋ Cheap (free to senior citizens and students under 19)
🔁 Fort St Elmo (➤ 38)
❓ The Wartime Experience (➤ 41) and the Lascaris War Rooms (➤ 38) are of related interest

---

✚ 35D4
✉ Republic Square
🍴 Eddie's Café Regina (£) (➤ 92)
♿ Good
🔁 All places of interest in Valletta are within walking distance

---

✚ 35F4
✉ Mediterranean Street
☎ 243840
🕐 Mon–Fri 9:30–4
🍴 Café (£) on the premises
✋ Cheap
🔁 Fort St Elmo and National War Museum (➤ 38 and above)
❓ Conducted tours

The Maltese suffered stoically in World War II and the award of the George Cross paid tribute to their endurance

ST PAUL'S SHIPWRECK ✪✪

Originally designed by Gerolamo Cassar in the 16th century, it underwent extensive modifications and gained a number of adornments that are now its chief attractions. These include ceiling frescoes, an altarpiece by the Florentine artist Paladini, and a piece of St Paul's wristbone behind a glass case on an altar. Another altar contains part of the block on which St Paul is said to have been beheaded, to be seen indistinctly from a distance. The statue of St Paul, by Melchiorre Gaffa, is carried through the streets on 10 February, the day St Paul's shipwreck is commemorated.

<hr>

➕ 35D3
✉ Triq San Pawl (St Paul's St)
☎ 222348
🕐 Mon–Fri 11–12:45 and 4–6, Sat 11–midday and 4–6
🍴 Cafés and restaurants (£) within walking distance
♿ None
🆓 Free
↔ Bibliotheca (➤ 32), Republic Square (➤ 40)

UPPER BARRACCA GARDENS ✪✪

These 18th-century gardens on top of St Peter and St Paul's demi-bastion, were planned as a roofed playground for Italian knights but the arches are the only reminder that the place was once covered. Now open to the air, the gardens offer excellent views of the Grand Harbour and Vittoriosa across the water and they also provide one of the best places for a picnic in Valletta. The gardens are dotted with statues, the most interesting being Sciortino's *Les Gavroches.*

<hr>

➕ 35D2
✉ Castile Place
🍴 Cafés and restaurants (£) within walking distance
♿ Few
↔ Auberge de Castile et Léon (➤ 32)

WARTIME EXPERIENCE ✪✪✪

This 45-minute black and white film tells the gripping and harrowing tale of Malta's sufferings in the face of the heaviest blitz of World War II. The film is composed entirely of original footage, there is no better introduction to this memorable chapter in the island's history. The narrative is impressive, building to a climax as the Maltese gave themselves one more month before surrendering, only to be saved when the *Ohio* limped into Grand Harbour carrying vital supplies of food and fuel.

<hr>

➕ 35D4
✉ Hostel de Verdelin, Palace Square
☎ 247891
🕐 Mon–Fri on the hour from 10–3, Sat 10, 11, 12
🍴 Cafés and restaurants (£–££) within walking distance
♿ None
🆓 Cheap
↔ Palace of the Grand Masters (➤ 21), Casa Rocca Piccola (➤ 32)
❓ The Valletta Experience (➤ 111) is presented in the same building

---

Did you know ?

Malta was the most heavily and most consistently bombed target in World War II. The people and the island were awarded the George Cross for 'Heroism and a Devotion that will long be famous in History'. The medal in the War Museum is said to be the original but rumour has it that the real medal is under lock and key elsewhere.

Around Malta

This small island has a deceptively large number of places worth seeing, so much so that visitors need to make choices about where to go and what to see. If sea, sand and a lively nightlife is a priority then head for St Julian's and Paceville on the north coast. A plethora of tourist hotels and restaurants cater to an annual invasion of those seeking entertainment, a Mediterranean ambience and a suntan. On a smaller scale is the fishing village of Marsaskala on the eastern side. One can travel around easily and visitors seeking a sense of the past should visit the ancient capital of Mdina, for few places in Europe evoke the medieval era so effortlessly.

'For there is every variety of luxury,
animal, mineral and vegetable—
a Bishop and daughter,
pease and artichokes, works in
marble and fillagree, red mullet,
and Archdeacon, Mandarin
Oranges, Admirals and Generals,
Marsala Wine 10d a bottle –
religious processions, poodles,
geraniums, balls, bacon, baboons,
books and what not.'

EDWARD LEAR
Letter to Lady Waldegrave (13 February 1866)

What to See Around Malta

ATTARD ✪✪

✚ 28C3
✉ 7km southwest of Valletta
🍴 Corinthia Palace Hotel (£–££)
🚌 40, 74
♿ Good
↔ Balzan & Lija (see below)

Visitors are allowed closer access to the president's residence than would be the case for most European heads of state

Attard and the neighbouring villages of Balzan and Lija (see below) are known collectively as the Three Villages, but it is Attard that has the chief claim to fame. Historically, it is associated with the 17th-century Grand Master Antoine de Paule, a hedonist who is infamously linked with the decline of the Order of St John into decadence. His summer residence near Attard, San Anton Palace, is now the official residence of Malta's president. Although its interior cannot be visited, the San Anton Gardens are open to the public. In Attard itself St Mary's Church is a splendid example of Renaissance church architecture, designed by Tommaso Dingli when he was only 22 years old. There is also an art gallery and pottery shop (➤ 107) in the vicinity.

BALZAN AND LIJA ✪

✚ Balzan 29D3, Lija 28C3
✉ 7km southwest of Valletta
🍴 Il-Melita (£, ➤ 93)
🚌 40
♿ None
↔ Attard (see above)

These two adjoining villages, just a short walk north of Attard, are of interest principally because of their churches. In Balzan the Church of the Annunciation and the Church of St Roque, dating back to the late 16th century, are both well preserved. Lija's Church of St Saviour looks uninspiring from the outside, but on a Sunday morning the late 17th-century painted interior can be appreciated. A 10-minute walk away in St Saviour Street is the Tal-Mirakli Church (Our Lady of Miracles), said to be sited in the exact geographical centre of Malta. It was rebuilt in the 17th century and has a fine altarpiece by Mattia Preti.

BIRKIRKARA ⊙

Visitors tend to just drive through the urban sprawl of Birkirkara and indeed from the window of a vehicle it does not seem very inviting. Among the numerous churches is the Collegiate Church of St Helen, the largest on Malta and a notable example of ecclesiastical baroque architecture. The exterior has a striking façade and entablature while inside are some beautiful and graceful frescoes. In the older part of town there is still a lot of character in the confusing maze of streets and houses.

BIRŻEBBUĠA ⊙⊙

Despite the seaside setting, Birżebbuġa is not recommended as a resort – the water is sometimes polluted – but its prehistoric cliff cave of Għar Dalam and museum are well worth seeing. The cave was first inhabited by stone age humans around 4000 BC (and the last occupants evicted in 1911) but excavations have revealed animal bones that go back some quarter of a million years: dwarf elephants, bears and hippopotamuses. More remains of animals have been found that may have lived within a cave only 145m long; the cave somehow functioned as a natural trap for both dead and live animals.

BLUE GROTTO ⊙⊙

The Blue Grotto experience is a half-hour trip along the coast by colourfully painted boat from Wied-iż-Żurrieq, passing through a series of natural sea caves with picturesque rock formations. Its popularity with tour coaches can mean waiting in a queue, so try to arrive early in the morning.

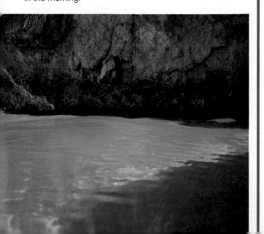

✚ 29D3
✉ 6km southwest of Valletta
🍴 Better to eat in Attard or Lija
🚌 41, 42, 71,78
♿ Few
↔ Attard, Balzan and Lija

✚ 29E1
✉ 10km southeast of Valletta. Għar Dalam is 1km north of Birżebbuġa
🕐 Mon–Sat 8:15–5, Sun 8:15–4:15
🍴 Restaurant (£–££) at the Sea Breeze hotel in nearby Pretty Bay
🚌 11, 115
♿ None
💷 Cheap
↔ Marsaxlokk (► 55)

✚ 29D1
✉ Wied-iż-Żurrieq, 3km southwest of Żurrieq
🕐 Daily 8–4
🍴 Cafés (£) between the car park and the sea
🚌 39, 32, 34
♿ None
💷 Cheap
↔ Qim & Mnajdra (► 18), Qrendi (► 64), Żurrieq (► 79)

The beautiful Blue Grotto

28B2
 4km south of Rabat
 Light refreshments available but a picnic is recommended
 81 Few
 Free
 Clapham Junction (see below), Dingli Cliffs (➤ 49), Verdala Palace (➤ 73)

 28B2
 0.5km south of Buskett Gardens
 81
 None
 Free
 Buskett Gardens (see above), Dingli Cliffs (➤ 49), Verdala Palace (➤ 73)

 83F2
 Comino Hotel (££)
 From Malta and Gozo
 None

BUSKETT GARDENS

These woodland gardens were created under Grand Master Lascaris in the 17th century with the practical purpose of raising hunting falcons. Today they offer welcoming shade during the heat of the summer. The name is taken from *boschetto* ('little wood') and the gardens reveal a botanically diverse collection of trees, including pine and oak as well as groves of oranges and olives. It is the perfect place to picnic and many Maltese families do just that at weekends. It is the only woodland area on the island.

CLAPHAM JUNCTION

A network of cart ruts, parallel grooves cut into the rock, that sometimes cross each other like railway lines was named by the British after a busy London rail interchange. It is not known when or why they came into being. While it is generally thought that Bronze Age (2000–1000BC) people made them with some kind of non-wheeled vehicles, there are other hypotheses, including one that attributes them to the Carthaginians and their iron-rimmed wheeled carts. The ruts vary in depth (40–60cm) and width which gives credence to the idea that they were created by wooden sleds made of tree trunks, tipped with iron runners, used to transport heavy goods and materials.

Cart ruts are found in various places in both Malta and Gozo but the largest concentration of them is here. They are signposted but when you reach the site it takes a few minutes to establish their presence. Once they are identified they take on an air of mystery. Why are they in this particular location, why do they converge, why do some disappear over the cliff edge and why are there so many?

COMINO

Comino is a small – 2.5km by 2km – virtually uninhabited island sandwiched between Malta and Gozo. There are no cars or roads and only one hotel (➤ 100) that opens for the summer. The island's history is unremarkable for it seems that only pirates were attracted to its coves and creeks and in 1618 Grand Master Wignacourt put an end to that by having a promontory fort, Comino Tower, built on Comino's west side.

Unless resident at the hotel, visitors come for a day trip to enjoy the crystal-clear turquoise water or slow walks in the fresh air along vehicle-free pathways (and it is impossible to get lost!). The whole island is a wildlife sanctuary but botanically, the island is not as interesting as might be hoped, and it is not easy to find the cumin plant (*kemmuna*) from which the island receives its name. If staying on the island, there are excellent diving possibilities and even daytrippers can enjoy snorkelling if they bring their own gear. The hotel offers a good range of water sports.

The only significant beach area is the Blue Lagoon, formed by a channel that separates sun-baked and barren Comino from the islet of Cominotto, and only the density of bathers detracts from the intrinsic beauty of this lagoon with its fine white sand. It is essential to arrive on Comino as early as possible, especially if you want to enjoy the Blue Lagoon. Be sure to bring protective clothing, cold drinks and a picnic, although food and drinks are available at the hotel.

Be sure to arrive early to enjoy the pleasures of Comino Island

West and Southwest Malta Drive

Distance
20km

Time
4–6 hours depending on visits to places of interest

Start point
Čirkewwa
 28A6

End point
Rabat & Mdina
 28B3

Lunch
Charles il-Barri (£–££)
✉ Mġarr, next to the church
☏ 573235

This is a chance to explore another side of Malta.

From Valletta, drive to Čirkewwa on the Gozo side of the isolated Marfa Peninsula. From Čirkewwa follow the road back to Valletta until a right turn is signposted for Golden Bay and Manikata. On the road to Manikata a vista of sea suddenly appears and after 3km turn right at the unsignposted T-junction for Golden Bay.

Detour to Golden Bay, a popular family beach. After a quick swim or lie in the sun, carry on.

After less than 1km, at another T-junction, turn right and then straight on for Għajn Tuffeħa (➤ 49). Return to the main road and turn right, looking for a small sign on the right after 1.5km for the Roman Baths (➤ 49). After another 0.5km a detour may be made to Mġarr (➤ 61).

Look at the 'Egg Church' and perhaps make a stop here and have lunch – the return journey is under 2km – the main road goes on to Żebbieħ and the Skorba Temples (➤ 61).

From Żebbieħ head for Mdina (➤ 71) and then follow the signs for the Dingli Cliffs (➤ 49). Turn left at the coast, keeping the Mediterranean on your right until the road swings inland. After 1.5km take the left turn at the roundabout, signposted for Rabat, and look for an unmarked crossroads with a church on the left. A left turn at this junction leads to Verdala Palace (➤ 73).

Stop for a tour of this cool palace if open.

Just 1km after the Palace the first turn left leads to Buskett Gardens (➤ 46), a sign points the way on to Clapham Junction (➤ 46).

Stretch your legs, and let yourself become absorbed in the mystery of the cart ruts. Then take the main road to Rabat.

DINGLI CLIFFS ✪✪
The village of Dingli, 253m above sea level, is the highest on Malta and the nearby Dingli Cliffs offer one of the island's most stunning panoramic views. The Mediterranean appears as a vast expanse with the islet of Filfla lost out on its own. On the edge of the cliff stands the tiny and lonely chapel of St Maġdalena that dates back to 1646. Most visitors arrive in their own transport (although a bus serves Dingli village and it is a short walk to the cliffs), but the location can only be really appreciated by leaving your vehicle and taking a stroll.

☩ 28B2
✉ 15km southwest of Valletta, 4km south of Rabat
🍴 Bobbyland Bar and Restaurant (➤ 94)
🚌 81   ♿ Few
↔ Verdala Palace (➤ 73)

The fine beach at Għajn Tuffieħa is rarely crowded

GĦAJN TUFFIEĦA AND GOLDEN BAY ✪✪
The two sandy beaches of Għajn Tuffieħa and Golden Bay, separated by a small headland, have military associations. It was in Għajn Tuffieħa that the Turkish fleet gathered before beginning the Great Siege of 1565, and the British trained their naval forces in both bays during World War II. Today, they attract mostly sun worshippers but the excavated Roman Baths nearby reveal a shared concern with the serious pursuit of leisure. The baths belonged to a Roman villa, now largely disappeared but the baths were renovated by Unesco in 1961 to show a complex that consisted of warm and cold baths, a hot-air room with underground heating and a separate small swimming pool. Occasional northwest winds create dangerous currents in the deeper parts of both bays and a red warning flag indicates the need to remain in the shallow part of the water.

☩ 28A4
Roman Baths
✉ Roman Baths are 1.5km from Għajn Tuffieħa on the road to Mġarr
🕐 Access is through advance notice to the Museums Department (☎ 251874) but it is possible to look through the fenced railings.
🍴 Golden Sands Hotel (£–££)
🚌 47 and 52 from Valletta, 51 from Buġibba and 652 from Sliema
♿ None
🎟 Free

49

+ 29D4

St Bartholomew's Church
- ✉ 7km northwest of Valletta
- ⏰ Mon–Sat 4–7:30, Sun 6–11:30 & 4–7:30
- 🍴 Refreshments (£) at the King George VI bar next to the church
- 🚌 55
- ♿ None
- ↔ Naxxar (▶ 62), Victoria Lines (▶ 73)

+ 34B5

Marsamxett Harbour
- ✉ Between Sliema and Valletta
- 🍴 Cafés and restaurants (£) within walking distance on the mainland seafront
- 🚌 60, 61, 62 to Yacht Marina and then across the bridge
- ♿ None
- ↔ Sliema (▶ 72)

GĦARGĦUR

This small village, subdued and picturesque, is hidden away at the top of a ridge, and manages unintentionally to evoke a sense of Malta's medieval past. If driving from Valletta, the turning off the main road is signposted for Madliena just before the Splash Park (▶ 109) and the uphill trip to Għargħur is like a journey into the sealed-off past as the road winds its way over an old viaduct and up into the sun-baked countryside. The town's church of St Bartholomew was designed by Tommaso Dingli in 1636 and its gloomy interior does little to detract from Għargħur's air of antiquity.

Għargħur marks the northern end of the Victoria Lines and nearby Fort Madliena is part of this defensive system. From Għargħur take a walk or drive inland to enjoy the spectacular scenery of the indented coastline, as well as views of the Great Fault that cuts off this corner of Malta.

GRAND HARBOUR (▶ 17, TOP TEN).

ĦAL-SAFLIENI HYPOGEUM (▶ 19, TOP TEN).

MANOEL ISLAND

Connected to the mainland by a bridge, Manoel Island has an unfortunate history that seems to continue to bedevil attempts to cash in on its unquestionably prime location. The Knights of Malta used the island as a quarantine station during plagues, when it eventually could deal with up to 1,000 people at a time. The British used it as a hospital until 1940 when it then became a submarine base. Heavy bombing took its toll of Fort Manoel which was constructed in 1732 to guard **Marsamxett Harbour**, but there are plans to renovate this highly impressive fort. In the meantime, the best reason for being on the island is to visit the Phoenician Glass Factory (▶ 106).

Did you know ?

Malta's rigid quarantine laws made no exceptions for famous visitors. Coleridge, Thackeray and Sir Walter Scott all suffered a period of incarceration on Manoel Island which could last from 18 to 80 days, depending on where they came from. Lord Byron was especially displeased: 'Adieu, thou damned'st quarantine, that gave me fever, and the spleen.'

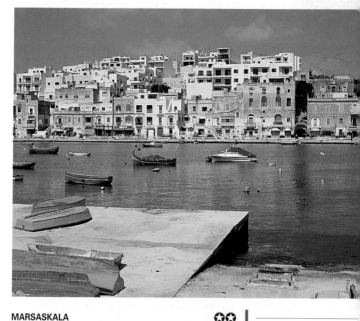

MARSASKALA ✪✪

The postcard-pretty harbour of Marsaskala witnessed the last Turkish assault on Malta in 1614. Although the troops landed they were beaten back while heading inland and the Knights quickly built a mighty fort on the nearby headland to deter any future visit. Today, a tourist infrastructure is developing apace and Marsaskala welcomes visitors with open arms. Appropriately enough, part of the fort's location has been turned into the area's premier tourist hotel, the Jerma Palace Hotel, and the fort is a restaurant. The village of Marsaskala has an agreeable setting by the water's edge with plenty of cafés and good seafood restaurants overlooking the bay and its pastel-coloured boats. In recent years the nightlife scene has become increasingly popular with visitors and Maltese alike. Between them, the bars and discos and an up-to-date cinema and restaurant complex appeal across the age range.

There is no beach, but nearby St Thomas Bay, 1km to the south, has sandy banks and shallow water. In summer it can seem too busy, but it is easy to escape the crowds by heading south along the coast towards Delimara Point. The road to St Thomas Bay from Marsaskala passes Mamo Tower, a 17th-century tower with an interesting cruciform design and just one room with a vaulted roof. It was privately built by a landowner to deter slave-collecting expeditions from North Africa dropping by in St Thomas Bay and abducting his peasants.

✚ 29F2
✉ 9km southeast of Valletta
🍴 Cafés and restaurants (£–££) by the seafront
🚌 19, 22
♿ Few
↔ Marsaxlokk (➤ 55), Zabbar (➤ 78)

The delightful resort of Marsaskala has developed across a narrow inlet on the southern coast

51

In the Know

If you only have a short time to visit Malta and Gozo, or would like to get a real flavour of the island, here are some ideas:

10
Ways To Be A Local

Show some respect for the virtue of patience; absolute punctuality is a worrying trait.

Take time off for an idle stroll along a promenade, Italian style, during the early evening hours.

Risk a flutter on one of the lotteries, like Super 5, and check the results on television or in the next morning's newspaper.

Greet people or say farewell with *sahha* (literally 'wish you good health').

Enjoy pastizzi for a morning break or late night repast.

Browse the markets and mingle with locals buying their fruit, vegetables, clothes and bric-à-brac.

Observe modest dress and behaviour in places of worship.

Relax and chat in a bar at any time of the day or night.

Let time pass over a light meal of bread, olive oil, tomatoes, vinegar and garlic in a café.

Do not refer to the people of Gozo as Maltese; they are Gozitans.

10
Good Places To Have Lunch

Cafe Ranieri (£) A popular brightly lit restaurant in the centre of Valletta with set meals, snacks, ice-creams, salads, pasta and pizza. Suitable for children.
✉ 39 Republic St, Valletta ☎ 249063 ⊙ Daily 8:30–8

China House (££) Easy to find on Spinola Road, this well-established Chinese restaurant has a reputation for reliability and large portions. The menu is vast.
✉ 8 Spinola Rd, St Julian's ☎ 335021 ⊙ Mon–Fri, Sun 12–2:30, 7–11

Clouds Restaurant (£–££) An American-style restaurant in the centre of Paceville that offers an atmosphere more relaxing at lunchtime than late at night. For a fast-food place the dishes are surprisingly tasty. Good ice-cream and milk shakes. ✉ St George's Road, Paceville, St Julian's ☎ 319646 ⊙ Mon–Sat 12–1AM (late at weekends)

It-Tmun (££) Close to the Xlendi seafront in Gozo, this relaxing restaurant is ideal for a slow lunch. The home-made soups are very good. Outside tables offer shade. ✉ 3 Mount Carmel Street, Xlendi, Gozo ☎ 551571 ⊙ Wed–Mon 12–2, 6–10

La Cave (£) In the basement of the Castile Hotel in Valletta it has a medieval atmosphere; the stone walls were built in the late 16th century. The fare is pizza and pasta, cooked well, and there is a very good wine list.
✉ Castile Hotel, Castile Square, Valletta ☎ 243677 ⊙ Mon–Fri, 12–3, 6–11:30

MLP Club (£) Scruffy décor and four plastic tables outside on a narrow verandah, but this is still a pleasant place to sit and enjoy an inexpensive meal of mussels, swordfish or toasted sandwiches.
✉ Spinola Square, St Julian's ☎ 337757 ⊙ 5:30AM–11PM

The Plough and Anchor (££) A small pub restaurant next to the Carlton Hotel on Tower Road (though the postal address is Main Street), with a nautical theme. English and Italian dishes cooked well.
✉ 1 Main Street, St Julian's ☎ 334725 ⊙ Tue–Mon 12–2:30, 6–10

Ponte Vecchio (££) A friendly well-established restaurant with outdoor tables and a menu that mixes Italian with Maltese dishes. The home-made pumpkin soup is delicious.
✉ 31 Stella Maris Stret, Sliema ☎ 341591 ⊙ Mon–Sat 12:30–2:30, 7–10:30 🚌 60, 61, 62, 63, 64, 67, 68 from Valletta, 70 from Buġibba, 65 from Rabat, 86 from Buġibba and Rabat, 645 from Ċirkewwa
🚢 Valletta–Sliema ferry (☎ 335689)

Porto del Sol (££–£££) Splendid views across Xemxija Bay and carefully cooked fish, pasta and meat dishes in a comfortable and formal restaurant. Good food and good wine.
✉ Xemxija Road, St Paul's Bay ☎ 573970

🕐 Mon–Sat 12–2:30, 7–11

Xerri il-Bukkett (£) Terrific views of Comino and Malta from a Gozo restaurant that offers nourishing home cooking. Indoor and outdoor tables. ✉ 4 Zewwieqa Road, Qala, Gozo ☎ 553500 🕐 Tue–Sun 12–3, 6–11

10
Top Activities

A day trip to Mount Etna in Sicily.

Fishing off a boat in Marsaxlokk or St Paul's Bay.

Hiring a bicycle in Marsalforn to explore the country roads of Gozo.

Hiring a car for a day to explore the southwest corner of Malta.

Jumping off the rocks into the deep blue sea.

Learning to water ski or dive in St Julian's.

Swimming in the Blue Lagoon on Comino Island early in the morning.

Taking a cruise around the Grand Harbour and admiring the sheer size of it (➤ 17).

Walking in Gozo, especially in the Ta'Cenc area (➤ 87).

Walking the Victoria Lines (➤ 73).

10
Best Beaches

Armier Beach. Situated in the extreme northeast of Malta (bus 50 from Valletta), with few facilities and occasional rough swells but lots of sand.

Comino's beaches. The Blue Lagoon (➤ 12) is deservedly the most popular spot.

Għajn Tuffieħa Bay. Less-crowded than Golden Bay beach yet only a short walk away and reached by steps (➤ 49)

Golden Bay. The most popular beach on the island after Mellieħa Bay because of its extensive stretch of sand (➤ 49).

Għejna Bay. Without your own transport there is a 2-km walk from Malta's Mġarr, but the worthwhile reward is sand with rocky platforms.

Marsaskala and St Thomas Bay. There is no sand but coastal bathing is very popular here because of the bay's picturesque location.

Mellieħa Bay. Malta's most popular beach is 2km north of Mellieħa. Shallow water and lots of sand make it entirely suitable for children.

Peter's Pool. Not much of a beach but a terrific jumping-off point into crystal-clear, deep water.

Ramla Bay. The only really sandy beach in Gozo, shallow and safe for swimming.

Sliema/St Julian's. No sand but there are plenty of rocky platforms for sun-bathing.

10
Best Drinks and Snacks

Drink

Averna. Recommended to settle the stomach after an indulgent heavy meal.

Bajtra The word is Maltese for prickly pear, where this very sweet liqueur comes from. Drink when chilled.

Fernet Branca. Like averna, this is a 'digestive drink' taken after eating a big meal. Swallow whole, tastes foul.

Kinnie. Malta's very own herbal soft drink.

Tamakari. One of the island's most popular liqueurs. Try a tamakari kinnie cocktail, – just the liqueur diluted with kinnie – ideally before an evening meal.

Food

Bigilla. Bread with crushed garlic and broad beans. Sold in packets from street carts.

Figolli. Iced biscuits with almond and lemon, usually only available at Easter time.

Gozo cheese, known as *gbejna*. The peppered version is the best, though some eat the unpeppered cheese for breakfast.

Maltese bread. Absolutely delicious if eaten freshly baked. If you are up early enough purchase it from the mobile breadman.

Pastizzi. Small savoury puff pastries filled with either local cheeses or peas.

MARSAXLOKK ★★

This is the largest fishing village on Malta, and the traditional and strong sense of community suggest it will remain so. Both the Turks in 1565 and Napoleon in 1798 landed their troops here and now there is an annual summer invasion of tourists but Marsaxlokk retains its character and appeal. Each Sunday morning the quayside becomes an open-air fish market, and throughout the week good seafood restaurants (➤ 95) serve the local catch.

There is no beach but interesting walks include a stroll to Delimara Point which passes a few bathing inlets on its eastern side. Heading south, a pleasant walk hugs the coastline as far as Birżebbuġa and takes in Għar Dalam en route.

- 🔲 29E2
- ⊠ 10km southeast of Valletta
- 🍴 Cafés and restaurants (£–££) by the seafront
- 🚌 27 from Valletta, 427 from Bugibba, 627 from Paceville
- ♿ Few
- ↔ Birżebbuġa (➤ 45), Marsascala (➤ 51)

> ### *Did you know ?*
>
> *Every brightly coloured* luzzu *or fishing boat has the ever-watchful Egyptian Eye of Osiris painted on its high prow to ward off evil spirits. There may be a Catholic shrine on board as well, neatly symbolising the intertwining of cultures on Malta.*

MELLIEHA ★★

Mellieha's popular sandy beach – the largest in Malta – is 2km north of town. It attracted Turkish pirates which led to the village of Mellieha, which is set on a spur, being deserted in the mid-16th century. The town's present shape goes back to the 19th century when the steep main street, where houses cling to the rock, was laid out. Selmun Palace (➤ 101), a prominent castle with adjoining chapel, that dominates the area from up on the ridge, was built in the mid-18th century by Domenica Cathias. It was once owned by a charitable foundation which aimed to ransom Christian slaves who had been taken to the Barbary Coast. It is now a hotel. The heritage prize, however, goes to an ancient Marian grotto below, but near the parish church Our Lady of Victories, which has been a place of worship for centuries. The fresco of the Virgin Mary above the altar is said to have been painted by St Luke. The spring water in the Grotto is credited with medicinal powers. Mellieha has always been a favourite place for the Maltese, and is becoming popular with visitors.

- 🔲 28B5
- ⊠ 23km west of Valletta
- 🍴 A good choice (£–££) of cafés and restaurants
- 🚌 43, 44, 45 from Valletta, 48 from Buġibba and Ċirkewwa, 645 from Sliema and Ċirkewwa
- ♿ Few

Mdina and Rabat

High ground away from the coast made Mdina a natural site for a defensively minded community, and Bronze Age people were probably the first to settle here. The Phoenicians and Romans knew it respectively as Maleth and Melita while the Arabs built walls 190m high around the town they called Mdina, leaving the poorer people outside in an area that came to be known as Rabat. In the following centuries Mdina emerged as the island's capital and remained so until the Knights made Valletta the new capital in 1571.

Today, fortified medieval Mdina and Rabat should not be missed by any first-time visitor. Mdina's honey-coloured walls and narrow winding alleyways and Rabat's catacombs and Roman remains make any visit memorable.

What to See in Mdina and Rabat

58A2
Cafés and restaurants (£–££) in Mdina and Rabat
80, 81, 83, 84, 86 from Valletta, 65 from Sliema
Steps and narrow uneven surfaces

MAGAZINE STREET AND GREEK'S GATE ★★

Magazine Street, so called because munitions were once stored here, borders the western side of Mdina and, unless a tour group has arrived, there is a surprising air of tranquillity to the place. There are many fine details to appreciate in the old dwellings, and photographers, if the light allows, enjoy trying to capture in close-up the brass

Entering medieval Mdina through the Greek's Gate

knockers, the cut stone or the window mouldings. Greek's Gate is named after a small number of Greeks who came to Malta with the Knights from Rhodes and settled in this corner of Mdina. The walls of Greek's Gate are very old, dating back to Arab times. Just north of Greek's Gate is another breach in the wall, made in the 19th century for those travelling to Mdina by train. The old train station, now a restaurant (► 96), can be seen in the valley below.

MUSEUM OF ROMAN ANTIQUITIES ✪✪

Remains of a Roman town house were discovered just outside Mdina in 1881 and the museum is built over the site. For anyone interested in ancient Rome there are some excellent exhibits. Downstairs these include some of the original mosaics that once adorned a floor in the house, surrounded by remains of columns and busts unearthed in different corners of Malta. Noteworthy exhibits in the main gallery include an olive crusher, discovered at Marsaxlokk, used to extract the pips so oil could be made from the pulp. There is also a 2nd-century tombstone recording the death of a comedian and musician and various smaller finds.

🖪 56B2
✉ Wesgha Tal-Muzew, Rabat
☎ 454125
🕐 16 Jun–30 Sep: Mon–Sun 8–2. 1 Oct–15 Jun: Mon–Sat 8–2, Sun 8–4
♿ Few
💶 Cheap

PALAZZO FALZON ✪✪

When Malta was under Spanish rule, from the late 13th century to the beginning of the 16th century, Maltese nobility first emerged and emulated the architecture of the Sicilian nobility (also under Spanish rule) when building their fine homes. This style, known as Siculo-Norman, is best represented by the Palazzo Falzon, in the design of the windows and the moulding – most notably over the two doorways. The first Grand Master received the keys to the city here. The ground floor is a small private museum with naval and harbour paintings. There are displays of antique furniture and 6th- and 17th-century kitchen utensils are displayed in the charming inner courtyard. This is a rare opportunity to look inside one of Mdina's great houses.

🖪 58B3
✉ Triq Villegaignon, Mdina
☎ 454512
🕐 Viewing by appointment
💶 No entrance fee but a donation is welcomed

PALAZZO GATTO MURINA ✪

This is one of the earliest examples of the Siculo-Norman style of architecture. Its well-preserved 14th-century façade still has the lamprey emblem of the Gatto Murinas.

🖪 58B3
✉ Gatto Murina St, Mdina

MDINA

0   50   100 m

58B3
Triq Villegaignon, Mdina

PALAZZO SANTA SOPHIA ✪

The date plaque of 1233 makes this the oldest building in Mdina. The ground floor is authentically medieval but the first floor, still true to the Siculo-Norman style, was added in 1938. Look up to the first floor level and you can see the typical horizontal moulded design known as a 'string course'. Across the road is the tiny church of St Roque, dedicated to the patron saint of diseases, which originally stood close to Mdina Gate. Grand Master de Vilhena probably did not like the idea of a church that attracted the sick, set so close to his residence, Palazzo Vilhena, so he had the first church taken apart and a new one built here.

Further up the road on the other side is the Carmelite Church, not architecturally significant, but possessing some historical worth in the story of the 1798 revolt against the French, which took place after the French confiscated valuable property from the church.

PALAZZO VILHENA/NATIONAL MUSEUM OF NATURAL HISTORY ✪

The magnificent Palazzo Vilhena, also known as the Magisterial Palace, was built by the Grand Master de Vilhena in the early 18th century. With a central courtyard, it was originally intended as his private residence. It later became an administrative building and the rear was turned into law courts, which in turn led to the basements being converted into a prison. The underground space has now been converted again to house the Mdina Dungeons (► 108). At the beginning of the 20th century the British turned the main building into a sanatorium, which it remained until the 1950s. It now houses the National Museum of Natural History with a large collection of geological finds, birds, insects, fossils and fauna. This is a good place to spend some time if your children are in the Mdina Dungeons.

➕ 58C2
✉ St Publius Square, on the right immediately after passing through Mdina Gate
☎ 455951 (Museum of Natural History)
🕓 16 Jun–30 Sep: Mon–Sun 7:45–1:30 1 Oct–15 Jun: Mon–Sat 8:30–4:30, Sun 8:15–3:30
💷 Cheap

ST AUGUSTINE'S CHURCH ✪

Gerolamo Cassar designed this church in 1571, just a couple of years before work began on his masterpiece in Valletta, and it is interesting to compare the two. Here, the grand Renaissance façade, rose windows and gilded, barrel-vaulted interior are among the features to admire.

➕ 56C1
✉ Triq Nikol Saura, Rabat
☎ 454111
🕓 Mass times 6:30–8AM, 5:30–6:30PM
💷 Free

ST PAUL'S AND ST AGATHA'S CATACOMBS (► 24, TOP TEN).

ST PAUL'S CATHEDRAL (► 25, TOP TEN).

ST PAUL'S CHURCH AND ST PAUL'S GROTTO ✪✪

The original church on this site was built in 1572 but most of what you now see belongs to the late 17th century when it was remodelled. The features worth noting include the altarpiece, designed by Mattia Preti and the paintings, among which is *The Shipwreck of St Paul* by Stefano Erardi. Underneath the church is a grotto that would be unremarkable save for the legend that St Paul found shelter in this place after his shipwreck.

➕ 56B1
✉ Pjazza Tal-Parocca, Rabat
☎ 454467
🕓 Daily 9:15–1:30, 2–5
💷 Free

St Paul's Church was the first on the island to be built to the design of a Latin Cross

A Mdina Walk

Distance
1km

Time
2–4 hours, depending on cathedral and other visits

Start point
Mdina Gate
✚ 58B2
🚍 80, 81, 83, 84, 86 from Valletta, 65 from Sliema

End point
Mdina Gate
✚ 58B2

Lunch
Fontanella Café (£)
✉ 1 Bastion Street
☎ 454264

The ancient streets of Mdina were not built for cars

The walk begins at the Mdina Gate and immediately after passing through the gate the Mdina Dungeons (► 108), a gruesome museum, is on the right. Next door is the Palazzo Vilhena and the National Museum of Natural History (► 59).

Turn left into Triq Inguanez, passing the entrance to the Mdina Experience (► 111) before reaching a T-junction with Triq L-Imhazen (Magazine Street) at the end of the street. Turn left for the Greek's Gate (► 56) but then continue back up Magazine Street (► 56) to Pjazza Tas-Sur (Bastion Square) at the top.

This was the old parade ground situated next to the main ramparts, and the strategic value of this vantage point becomes obvious when one looks over to see St Paul's Bay in the distance and the dome of Mosta's church (► 62). This is also the natural place to stop for lunch because various cafés (► 95–6) have outdoor tables up on the ramparts.

From Pjazza Tas-Sur walk down Triq Villegaignon, Mdina's main street, pass the Palazzo Falzon and the church of St Roque (► 58) before turning left for St Paul's Cathedral (► 59).

The cathedral, with its twin belfries, dominates Pjazza San Pawl. The site was, according to legend, where St Paul converted the governor, Publius, to Christianity.

After your visit, with the cathedral entrance behind you, turn to the left out of the square passing the Caffé Medina and back onto Triq Villegaignon.

Before reaching the Mdina Gate look for the historic Casa Inguanez on the left. The Inguanez family, the oldest noble family in Malta, have lived here since 1370.

What Else to See Around Malta

MĠARR   ✪

There are not many settlements in the southwest of Malta so the farming village of Mġarr (there is a harbour with the same name in Gozo) makes a useful stop for refreshments in the course of exploring this corner of the island. It is also very close to the prehistoric sites of Skorba and Ta'Ħagrat. The town's Church of the Assumption, called the 'Egg Church' has an interesting story. In the 1930s the local priest asked the villagers to donate eggs, that could be sold for a building fund. The villagers also donated their labour, which, explains why with no outside help, the building work lasted from 1912 to 1946.

✛ 28B4
✉ 16km northwest of Valletta
🕐 Church daily 6–11, 4–7
🍴 A good restaurant (£–££) next to the church
🚌 47
♿ Few

Mosta's church has one of the world's largest unsupported domes

61

✚ 28C3
✉ 8km west of Valletta
☎ 433826
🕐 Daily: 9–noon, 3–5
(religious services after
5PM)
🍴 Cafés and restaurants (£)
near the church
🚌 43, 44, 45, 49, 53, 56, 57
♿ Few
💰 Free
↔ Naxxar (➤ below)

✚ 29D3
✉ 3km southwest of
Valletta
🍴 Cafés and restaurants (£)
within walking distance
🚌 40–45, 47, 49, 50, 52, 53,
54, 56, 57, 60, 60–64, 68
♿ Few
↔ Valletta (➤ 30–41),
Sliema (➤ 72)

✚ 28C4
✉ 9km west of Valletta
🍴 Bars and cafés (£) across
the road from the church
🚌 54, 55, 56, 65
♿ Good
↔ Mosta (➤ above)

MOSTA

It is the immense parish church, the Mosta Rotunda, in this busy town in the centre of Malta that attracts visitors. The Rotunda, built in the mid-19th century, has massive walls up to 6m deep and these allowed the enormous dome – the fourth largest in Europe – to be constructed without scaffolding. This amazing building feat, which lasted 27 years, was helped by the older church on the same site which was only dismantled when the new church was complete. Some question the aesthetic harmony of the two belfries and the Ionic columns of the façade fronting such a large dome, but this cannot detract from the beautiful interior, with six side chapels, intricate marble floor and almost three-dimensional murals by Giuseppe Cali. The sacristy contains a replica of a 200kg bomb that pierced the dome in 1942 but failed to explode amidst the congregation. Two other bombs bounced off the dome without exploding.

MSIDA

This once small fishing village set in a creek of Marsamxett Harbour developed into a thriving town, helped in 1989 by the building of a yacht marina, now part of Matta's main yachting marina. The parish church of St Joseph is worth a visit for its two altarpieces by Guiseppe Cali. The Ta'Xbiex Seafront, where yachts berth, offers pleasant views of Floriana across the water. There are a multitude of cafés to choose from to sit and watch the world go by.

NAXXAR ○

The parish of Naxxar, on a commanding site, dates back to 1436 – one of the original 10 parishes – so while there may be some credence to the story that after his shipwreck St Paul came here and washed his clothes out (Naxxar translates as 'to hang clothes to dry') one might wonder why he trekked 8km from the coast to do so. Our Lady of Victories is a worthy but severe building designed by Tomasso Dingli in 1616.

The quiet suburb of San Pawl tat-Tarġa ('St Paul of the Step') where St Paul is said to have preached from steps of the church, is only 1km away. Near the church are two towers, the Gauci Tower and Torri tal-Kapitan, both now privately owned, built by the Knights of Malta in the mid-16th century. Naxxar's postition is now somewhat isolated.

The graceful baroque edifice of St Joseph's Church
dominates Msida Creek; the building was completed in 1892

QAWRA AND BUĠIBBA

The New Dolmen Hotel in Qawra captures the town's past and present: prehistoric remains in the grounds of an ultra-smart tourist hotel. If you are staying in either of these two tourist areas there are plenty of leisurely diversions including countless restaurants, shops and a number of bars and nightclubs. There are ambitious plans to redevelop the seafront and smarten up Buġibba, further increasing its attractiveness as an accomodation centre. The bigger hotels organise various water activities and there is an independent diving school as well as cruises from Buġibba's il-Menqa quay next to Bognor Beach. St Paul's Bay is a short walk away to the west along a coastal road. Buġibba is an important bus interchange with routes that manage to actually bypass Valletta.

✚ 28C5
✉ 15km northwest of Valletta
🍴 Plenty of cafés and restaurants (£–££)
🚌 49 from Valletta, 48 from Ċirkewwa, 51 from Għajn Tuffieħa, 70, 645, 652, from Sliema, 86 between Buġibba and Rabat, 427 between Buġibba and Marsaxlokk
♿ Good
⟷ St Paul's Bay (➤ 67)

WHAT TO SEE

✚ 29D3
✉ 4km southwest of Valletta
🍴 Nowhere suitable for a meal in the old part of town
🚌 88, 89, 90, 91
♿ The narrow streets are not wheelchair-friendly
↔ Valletta (➤ 30–41)

✚ 29D1
✉ 11km southwest of Valletta
🍴 Only a couple of bars (£)
🚌 35
♿ Good
↔ Ħagar Qim & Mnajdra (➤ 18), Blue Grotto (➤ 45), Żurrieq (➤ 79)

The village of Qrendi prepares for a festival procession

QORMI

Too many visitors travel past Qormi on their way to somewhere else, but they miss the town's medieval heritage which is reflected in the maze of very narrow streets and alleys in the old part of town, a little to the north of the modern town centre. Qormi was once known as Casal Fornaro meaning 'Village of Bakers'. There are no special sights, although the tall church of St George is a pleasing edifice with a well-proportioned exterior that balances its façade, spires and dome. This acts as a useful landmark while exploring the nearby winding streets where one is occasionally surprised by a lovely 16th-century house with an ornate balcony.

QRENDI ✪✪

This is the perfect village for those who like to seek out relatively unimportant places of antique interest. The diminutive church of St Catherine Tat-Torba is worth a visit if only to wonder at its unique façade. Another oddity, for Malta, is the octagonal Gwarena Tower, while to the south of the village there is a natural wonder known as Il-Maqluba. This huge hole in the soft limestone, some 100m across and 50m deep, was caused presumably by the collapse of a subterranean cave. This gave rise to an unflattering legend concerning the people of Qrendi: the inhabitants were so ungodly that they and their village were cast into hell, via Il-Maqluba, but even the devil rejected them and the tangled mass was cast into the sea thus creating the islet of Filfla.

North Coast Drive

The North Coast was where St Paul was shipwrecked and where both the Turks and Napoleon landed.

Follow Tower Road in Sliema in the direction of St Julian's, following the signs for St Paul's Bay and Mellieha.

Once outside town the first stopping point is the unsignposted village of Għargħur (➤ 50).

To reach it, turn left at the turning for Madliena which is signposted (if you pass Splash Park you have gone too far) and follow the winding road up to Għargħur.

Soak up the atmosphere of this ancient elevated village with fine views and enjoy a mid-morning drink in the tiny King George VI bar.

Retrace your route to the main road and turn left to continue travelling west towards St Paul's Bay.

The road hugs the coast as far as Salina Bay before reaching Buġibba and St Paul's Bay (➤ 67). A walk along the promenade in St Paul's should give one an appetite for lunch.

After lunch drive the short distance further west to Mellieħa (➤ 55), stopping perhaps at the island's largest sandy beach which is just 2km north of the town, descending the ridge. From the beach continue on to the northwest corner of Malta, the Marfa Ridge, and photogenic Ċirkewwa from where the ferries depart for Gozo.

There are a number of small beaches near here which, outside weekends, attract few visitors.

From Ċirkewwa head back to Mellieħa and turn right at the main roundabout to head south to Għajn Tuffieħa (➤ 65). From here take the main road to Żebbieħ, Mosta and Naxxar (➤ 62). From Naxxar it is a short distance back to Sliema.

Distance
40km

Time
6–8 hours

Start point
Sliema
🚗 20C4

End point
Sliema
➕ 29E4

Lunch
Gillieru Restaurant (££–£££)
☎ 573480

ST JULIAN'S, PACEVILLE AND ST GEORGE'S BAY ✪✪

St Julian's was a sleepy fishing village that awoke one day in 1798 to find nearly 500 of Napoleon's ships in the bay. The French invasion was largely unopposed and 200 years later a different kind of invasion takes place each summer when thousands of visitors of all nationalities visit. Their arrival is welcomed because St Julian's, sometimes seen as just an extension of Sliema, is a major tourist centre in its own right. It is attractively located along the line of the two curving bays of Balluta and St Julian's (sometimes called Spinola) and its promenade is a continuation of Tower Road in Sliema.

Beyond St Julian's is a small promontory where Paceville is located. Paceville (pronounced patchville) is the nightlife capital of Malta and when darkness falls neon lighting illuminates the discos, pubs and cafés that jostle for space and customers. At the tip of the promontory, Dragonara Point, is Malta's only casino (➤ 110), operating appropriately enough in what was once the summer residence of a wealthy banker.

Around the headland of Dragonara Point is St George's Bay, the only local beach area and consequently very popular. The sandy part of the beach is minute and, although the number of bobbing boats makes any kind of water activity difficult, the setting is very attractive and there are lidos nearby. The far side of St George's Bay is developing into a mass of top-notch hotels, which are dominated by the San Gorg hotel, and there are a number of quality restaurants.

ST PAUL'S BAY ✪✪

This premier resort area stretches from Mistra Bay on the west side of St Paul's Bay down to the mouth of the bay via Xemxija and up through Buġibba to Qawra on the east side of St Paul's. The sun, good beaches, beautiful water and sea-side fun atmosphere combine to make it a mass-market destination. The original village of St Paul's Bay covers the area between Għajn Razul and St Paul's Church, for the saint was shipwrecked here in AD 60. The elegant church of St Paul was built where he lit a bonfire and threw a viper into it, thus miraculously expelling all the poison from Malta's snakes. About 1.5km from the church, on the left side of the main road in the direction of Xemxija, is Għajn Razul (the Apostle's Fountain). Here St Paul baptised the first Maltese or, according to another legend, it is the site where he struck a rock and water poured forth. A Grand Master created the shrine and his coat of arms adorns the façade.

🔲 29D4
✉ 7km northwest of Valletta
🍴 Plenty of cafés and restaurants (£–£££) in the area
🚌 62, 64, 67, 68, 70 from Valletta, 627 between Paceville and Marsaxlokk
♿ Few
↔ Sliema (➤ 72)

St Paul's Bay (opposite) and Spinola Bay are home to two of Malta's premier resorts

---

🔲 28B5
✉ 19km northwest of Valletta
🍴 Plenty of cafés and restaurants (£–££) along the seafront
🚌 43, 44, 45, 49, 50 from Valletta, 48 from Ċirkewwa
♿ Good
↔ Qawra & Buġibba (➤ 63)

Food & Drink

Hotels and restaurants serve a large range of international cuisines ranging from Italian to the oriental, with a strong British contribution along the lines of roast beef and apple pie. Less ostentatiously displayed but well worth seeking out are the local establishments which serve the traditional home cooking of the islands.

Maltese Cuisine

Maltese food owes much to the many cultures of the peoples who have occupied or traded with the island over the centuries. Like Italian food it often uses pasta, and like Moorish food it relies on spicy sauces, but it has a quality of its own which has evolved from the special circumstances of the island. Many vegetables can be grown all year round while fish tends to be seasonal. The shortage of firewood for ovens in the past meant that food was cooked slowly in earthenware pots or taken to the village baker to be roasted. Despite the advent of modern stoves these styles of cooking are still preferred and they too influence the taste of the food.

Pastry is a common element. Combinations of meat or fish with vegetables and cheeses are encased in shortcrust or filo-type pastry. *Lampuki* pie is a

The simple pleasure of delicious fresh bread is a daily blessing in Malta and Gozo

must for anyone interested in Maltese food. It is available mainly in August because its chief element is the *dorado* (swordfish). This is mixed with spinach, cauliflower, chestnuts and sultanas and baked in shortcrust pastry. Another traditional pastry dish is the Sicilian *timpana*, a mixture of meat, liver, tomatoes, eggs and pasta with a pastry crust.

Traditional soups are often based on fish with garlic, tomatoes and marjoram. A traditional spring vegetable soup is *kusksu*, made from broad beans, pasta, and tomatoes.

Traditional meat dishes which should be tried include stewed rabbit cooked in wine and *bragioli*, little parcels of stuffing wrapped in slices of beef and slowly simmered.

Vegetable Dishes

Vegetarians can do well. The range of vegetables is extraordinary and because of the traditional abstinence from meat on Fridays many vegetable dishes are available. The Maltese version of ratatouille is called *kapunata*, a mix of garlic, aubergine and peppers. Savoury pumpkin pie is popular as well as spinach and anchovy pies. Widow's soup is a mixture of vegetables and goats' cheese (*Gbejna*). There is even a Maltese version of minestrone called *minestra* – made with at least eight vegetables – which is often more like a thick vegetable stew than its Italian counterpart. Accompanied by the excellent Maltese bread, soups make a satisfying meal.

Desserts and sweets are popular, sometimes spectacular, but rarely like the pastries of other European cuisines. On the street, especially during a festival, home-made nougat, iced biscuits stuffed with almond paste (*figoli*) or fresh fruit are sold. Another dish eaten during festivals is *prinjolata*, a dessert made from a pyramid of sponge fingers, almond cream, chocolate and cherries. Bakeries sell delicious filled pastries while restaurants offer *helwa tat-Tork* which is a crushed mix of sugar and almonds, or ice cream.

Wine, beer and soft drinks are readily available, including familiar international brands

Alcoholic Drinks

Local wine is cheap and mostly quite cheerful, but beware of the high alcohol content. Local beers are Hopleaf, and Blue Label and Cisk lager. Lowenbrau and Stella Artois are available. Even small cafés usually sell alcohol, and bars sell food and beverages.

28E3
4km (by road) south of Valletta
Café (£) near the church but consider a picnic
3
Good

SENGLEA ✪✪

Senglea, on a peninsula separating two waterways, is one of the historic Three Cities, along with Vittoriosa and Cospicua, where the Knights first settled after 1530. It was almost completely destroyed in World War II. The Safe Haven Gardens at the promontory's tip, the northern end of Victory Street, are worth a visit. From the lookout in the gardens there is a truly spectacular view of the Grand Harbour with Vittoriosa's Fort Angelo over to the right and Valletta's mighty walls straight across the water. The stone vedette at the tip carries a sculptured eye and ear, symbols of vigilance.

28C2
8km southwest of Valletta
A bar (£) in Siġġiewi serves snacks and there is a restaurant (£) at Għar Lapsi
89, 94
Few
Ħagar Qim (➤ 19), Buskett Gardens (➤ 46)

SIĠĠIEWI ✪✪

This village, one of 10 original parishes, had a population of 1,500 when the Knights arrived in 1530. It has one of the foremost baroque churches on the island. The dominating church of St Nicholas was built in the last quarter of the 17th century with two aisles and a dome added in the 19th century. The richly embellished interior includes an altar-piece that is the last, unfinished, work by Preti.

Under 5km to the west of Siġġiewi the attractively located Inquisitor's Summer Palace, built in 1625 by Inquisitor Visconti, may be viewed, but not visited as it is now a summer home for the prime minister. Some 4km to the south of Siġġiewi, on the coast, is Għar Lapsi. There is no sand but it is a popular swimming spot with Maltese families and there is a footpath to the Blue Grotto (➤ 45).

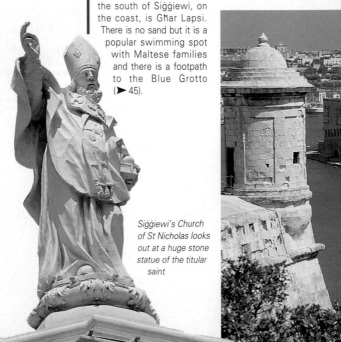

Siġġiewi's Church of St Nicholas looks out at a huge stone statue of the titular saint

SKORBA AND TA'ḤAĠRAT ✪

These two archaeological sites may appear to be just a collection of old stones, but both have revealed important clues to Malta's prehistory. The Skorba site was excavated in the 1960s and the finds of pottery, animal bones and wheat make it likely that this was a Neolithic and Bronze Age dwelling place. The site is permanently locked but one can peer through the railings.

The Ta'Ḥaġrat site, in the centre of Mġarr, revealed evidence of temples that are contemporary with Ġgantija. This makes it the earliest standing temple site in Malta, and both sites, with Ġgantija, are the oldest standing monuments in the world.

> ### *Did you know ?*
>
> *St Luke, who accompanied St Paul,*
> *recorded their arrival:*
> *'And the barbarous people [living near what is*
> *now St Paul's Bay] shewed us no little kindness:*
> *for they kindled a fire, and received us every*
> *one, because of the present rain and because of*
> *the cold.' Acts of the Apostles: 28: 1–2*

✚ 28B4

✉ Skorba is signposted on the left before Żebbieħ on the road from Mġarr Ta'Ḥaġrat is a short walk from the centre of Mġarr

🍽 A good restaurant (£) in Mġarr near the church

🚌 47

♿ Ta'Ḥaġrat may be viewed from the outside but Skorba is more difficult to approach

↔ Għajn Tuffieħa and Golden Bay (➤ 49)

❓ A key to Ta'Ḥaġrat is kept at the police station 100m up the road near the church (but the police station may be closed)

Senglea viewed across the Grand Harbour from a Valletta lookout

🏁 29E4

✉ 7km from Valletta

🍴 Plenty of cafés and restaurants (£–££)

🚌 60, 61, 62, 63, 64, 67, 68 from Valletta, 70 from Buġibba, 65 from Rabat, 86 from Buġibba and Rabat, 645 from Ċirkewwa, 652 from Golden Bay

⛴ Valletta-Sliema ferry (☎ 335689)

♿ Generally manageable along Tower Road and The Strand but the side streets are often steep and difficult to manage

↔ St Julian's, Paceville and St George's Bay (▶ 67)

Space on land, at least, is at a premium in upmarket Sliema (below). Not so at Popeye Village (opposite)

SLIEMA

Sliema is an affluent and fashionable residential area for the Maltese and a prime holiday base for tourists thanks to a number of top- and middle-range hotels. Tower Road is its 5-km promenade, full of shops and restaurants, and the road continues north to St Julian's and Paceville. Sliema has no sandy beaches but swimming and bathing off the rocky platforms along Tower Road is popular and there is a lido along the road. The southern end of Tower Road joins The Strand which fronts Sliema Creek. A short way along The Strand, at a transport point known as The Ferries, there is a bus terminus, a regular 5-minute ferry service to Valletta, Captain Morgan cruises to Comino and elsewhere (▶ 111), a hoverboat service to Gozo and, further down the road, the bridge to Manoel Island. From The Strand at night there are atmospheric views of Valletta across the water and it is always a popular place for Maltese residents to stroll and chat. The side streets into residential Sliema do not lead to any specific sights, but a meandering walk should throw up some of the fine villas built by the Maltese bourgeoisie at the beginning of the 20th century.

The Tigne headland offered the best point for guarding Marsamxett Harbour and Valletta, although the Knights did not build a fort here until 1792. Other forts are dotted along the coastline and one of them is now the Il-Fortizza restaurant on Tower Road.

SWEETHAVEN/POPEYE VILLAGE ✪

Hollywood came to Malta in 1979 and made *Popeye the Movie* around a set that was constructed at Anchor Bay to the west of Mellieha. The set created a 'Canadian' seaside village, Sweethaven, now a somewhat inappropriate tourist attraction. The dilapidated buildings are empty wooden constructs and the cardboard cutouts will hardly stir the imagination but young children may enjoy the spectacle. The tiny adjoining beach has rough sand.

✚ 28A5
✉ 1km west of Mellieha Bay at Anchor Bay
☎ 572430
🕐 Apr–Sep: daily 9–7; Oct–Mar: daily 9–5
🍴 Café (£)
🚌 44 or 45 to Mellieha Bay
♿ Manageable
🎟 Moderate
↔ Mellieha (➤ 55)

TARXIEN TEMPLES (➤ 26, TOP TEN)

VERDALA PALACE ✪

This castle-like palace was built in 1586 by a Grand Master as a summer residence and, now as a seasonal home for the president, performs a similar kind of function. It has been renovated and enriched over the centuries but the luxury of its interior cannot be seen by visitors unless it once again opens to the public on certain days of the week.

✚ 28C2
✉ 3km southeast of Rabat
🚌 81
↔ Buskett Gardens (➤ 46), Clapham Junction (➤ 46), Dingli Cliffs (➤ 49)

VICTORIA LINES ✪✪

There is a natural fault line running across Malta, the Great Fault, and the Knights were the first to capitalise on the defensive capabilities of this rift in the land that reaches 239m. They built watchtowers in gaps in the fault and later the British reinforced these, added more, and linked them up with a stonework parapet before officially christening them the Victoria Lines. Given their commanding position, the Victoria Lines offer scenic views across to Gozo and a focus for short walks in Malta's countryside. A recommended 3-km stretch is that between Nadur (west of Rabat) and Falka Gap, and the Lines can also be reached from Għargħur, Mġarr, Mosta and Naxxar.

✚ 28B4
✉ From Fomm ir-Rih (southwest of Mġarr) to Fort Madliena (northeast of Għargħur)
🍴 Bring a picnic or eat in Mġarr, Mosta or Naxxar (£–££)
🚌 46, 47 to Mġarr, 49, 53, 56 to Mosta, 55 to Għargħur and Naxxar
♿ None

Vittoriosa

In 1530 the Knights of the Order of St John chose a settlement on a narrow peninsula of land overlooking the creeks of the Grand Harbour as their headquarters, and set about fortifying it. Then known as Birgu, in 1565 the town was besieged for three months by the Turks and, though many lives were lost, the town was not taken. After the siege the Knights began the construction of a new capital but Birgu was given the name Vittoriosa – the victorious one – as an accolade. Many of the early buildings and fortifications of the Knights are still here along with narrow winding streets, and there are many reminders of the second great siege during World War II.

What to See in Vittoriosa

CHURCH OF ST LAWRENCE ●●

Originally built in the 11th century, this historically important church was rebuilt in 1530 by the Knights of St John as their Conventual Church. In 1691 it was virtually reconstructed by Lorenzo Gafa (builder of the cathedrals at Mdina and Victoria on Gozo) in the baroque style. The well balanced and impressive exterior with twin clock towers and dome is matched by a lavish dimly-lit interior. The church was damaged during World War II but the reconstruction and repairs are faithful to the original. Red marble and frescoes by Cortis and Joseph Calli adorn the walls and the ceiling. The most important work displayed in the chapel is a depiction of the martyrdom of St Lawrence by Mattia Preti.

The hat and sword of Grand Master La Valette are exhibited in the chapel of the Church of St Lawrence

✚ 35F1
✉ Triq San Lawrenz, Vittoriosa
☎ 827057
🕐 Mon–Sun 6–10, 4–7
🍴 The Old City Pub (£) (▶ 99)
🚌 1, 2, 4, 6
♿ Good
💷 Free
❓ Festival of St Lawrence 10 August

A Walk in Vittoriosa

The old capital has both impressive sites and tiny, homely stores and shops on this important promontory in Grand Harbour.

Enter Vittoriosa through the main gate, the Gate of Provence, which leads directly to the main street, Triq il-Mina-Kbira.

On the right the Inquisitor's Palace (➤ 77) is passed and soon after the street enters Victory Square (➤ 77).

Keep on your left for St Joseph's Oratory (➤ 77) and take the first turning out of the Square on the left and down some steps for St Lawrence's Church (➤ 74).

With your back to the church entrance, turn right at the water's edge and pass through the gate (The Old City Pub is to the left on the quayside), pausing to admire the splendid Canaletto-like view across the water.

Passing the Maritime Museum (➤ 77) on the right, walk along the quayside past the boats and ships and cross the small bridge at the end before walking up the broad ramp to Fort St Angelo (➤ 76).

Stop to admire the views on both sides and maybe take a photograph.

Retrace your steps to Victory Square and, from the position where you first entered the Square along Triq il-Kbira, take the narrow turning in the right corner (which has a street sign saying Block 5) signposted for the auberges.

The *auberges* (none open) were the first, more humble, ones of the Order. Go straight down this narrow lane, passing the Auberge d'Angleterre on the right.

At the end bear to the right and follow the street uphill until a fork is reached. Bear to the right and go along this street, Pacifiku Scicuna, to the end where you turn right at the T-junction. Then take the next left to enter once more the main street, Triq il-Kbira, which leads back to the gate where you entered Vittoriosa.

A fine example of vernacular architecture in Victory Square in Vittoriosa

Distance
1.5km

Time
2–4 hours, depending on church and museum visits

Start point
Main gate entrance to Vittoriosa
✚ 35F1
🚌 1, 2, 4, 6

End point
Main gate entrance to Vittoriosa
✚ 35F1

Lunch
The Old City Pub (£)
✉ Quayside
☎ 663614
❓ A tourist board brochure, *A Walking Tour of the Cottonera*, includes a map of Vittoriosa

35F1
Vittoriosa Wharf
Closed to the public
The Old City Pub (£)
1, 2, 4, 6
Free
Some uneven surfaces

FORT ST ANGELO

Records show that a fort called Castrum Maris stood on the site of Fort Angelo in 1274 but it is believed that a building was here long before that, possibly a temple to the Phoenician goddess Asthart. In 1530 it became the seat of the Grand Master and the Knights added more fortifications which withstood the Great Siege. When the siege ended the great bell was rung continuously for a day. Later the fort became a prison where rebellious Knights were held. There are two chapels inside the fortress, one a 12th-century building dedicated to the Virgin Mary and the other a 16th-century building dedicated to St Anne. The early Grand Masters are buried here, as are many of the knights who died defending the city. The fort was the British naval headquarters and the base for Allied naval operations in the Mediterranean during World War II.

The defences of Fort St Angelo are clearly visible from Valletta

THE INQUISITOR'S PALACE ○○
This building began its life in the Norman period as the Court of Justice but was enlarged and taken over when the Papal Inquisition came to Malta in 1574. The 62 Inquisitors sat here and an unknown number of people were tortured and died at their hands. Two of the Inquisitors went on to become popes, Alexander VII and Innocent XII. In the museum are exhibits of household utensils, tools, furniture and craft paraphernalia. The dungeons with prisoners' graffiti are still there, as are the courtrooms and the Inquisitors' chapel. One wing of the building dates back to the original Norman structure.

✚ 35F1
✉ Main Gate Street, Vittoriosa
🕐 Summer: Mon–Sun 7:45–2. Winter: Mon–Sat 8:15–4.30, Sun 8:15–4
🍽 The Old City Pub (£)
🚌 1, 2, 4, 6
♿ None
🎫 Cheap

THE MARITIME MUSEUM ○○
Built in 1842 as a bakery for the British Mediterranean Fleet, and in use as a store house until the British left in 1979, this building has been renovated and converted into a maritime museum. The walls are decorated with pictures of the hundreds of ships which have played a part in Malta's history while the various rooms effectively display different eras in naval history. There are Roman anchors, models of the ships of the Order of St John, Royal Navy vessels as well as models of the tiny *luzzu* which still bob about the harbour, medieval navigating equipment, cannon and ancient uniforms.

✚ 35F1
✉ Vittoriosa Wharf
☎ 660052
🕐 Summer: Mon–Sun 7:45–2. Winter: Mon–Sat 8:15–5, Sun 8:15–4:15
🍽 The Old City Pub (£)
🚌 1, 2, 4, 6
♿ None
🎫 Cheap

ST JOSEPH'S ORATORY ○○
This tiny, interesting museum was built in the 18th century as a chapel; it is now used as such once a year on 8 September, the anniversary of the retreat of the Turks. It is set in a little square outside the north door of the Church of St Lawrence. Exhibits include the hat and sword worn by Grand Master La Vallette, and curiosities ranging from long wafer-holding tongs used by the priests to give communion when there was a plague, an ancient crucifix used at public executions, and an early Bible used by the Inquisitors, to a much-used pack of playing cards of 1609.

✚ 35F1
✉ Vittoriosa Square
🕐 Mon–Sat 8:30–12, 2–4, Sun 9:30–12
🍽 The Old City Pub (£)
🚌 1, 2, 4, 6
♿ Few
🎫 Free

VICTORY SQUARE ○
This square was the centre of social life here in Vittoriosa for centuries. In it is the Victory Monument, erected in 1705, a statue of St Lawrence and a stone crucifix marking the spot where executions took place. On 10 August this square comes alive at the Festival of St Lawrence. Around the square are the *auberges* of Germany, England (which never moved to Valletta because of the Reformation) and Auvergne, but these *auberges* are modest compared to the grand ones in Valletta.

✚ 35F1
✉ Vittoriosa Square
🍽 The Old City Pub (£)
🚌 1, 2, 4, 6
♿ Good

What Else to See Around Malta

ŻABBAR

The Turks set up camp here on the dawn of the Great Siege, when the then village lay just outside the later Cottonera Lines, the fortified walls protecting the Three Cities, where the Knights first settled. When the French were blockaded behind the Lines in 1800 the village of Żabbar became the focus for the Maltese military opposition. French cannon fire did serious damage to the church of Our Lady of Graces but the restored church is worth a visit. Originally designed by Tommaso Dingli in 1640, the impressive ceiling of the nave is his only intact work. The exterior façade is a good example of over-the-top baroque. On Sunday mornings the church opens a small ecclesiastical museum with a number of votive paintings. East of town the Hompesch Arch, which is forlornly placed in the middle of a road junction, is a sad reminder of Malta's last Grand Master who surrendered to Napoleon.

> ### *Did you know ?*
> *Grand Masters ruled Malta from 1530 to 1798 but only the last one (1797–98), Ferdinand von Hompesch from Germany, bothered to learn the Maltese language. He was also the only German Grand Master. A weak leader, but a kind man, he learned the language because he respected the Maltese.*

ŻEBBUĠ

The town of Żebbuġ, one of the original 10 parishes of 1486, is indifferent to tourism and few visitors bother stopping other than those seeking out interesting old churches. The church of St Philip, built in 1632, in the town square is the most impressive place of worship, designed by the son of the famous Gerolamo Cassar who was so influential in the building of Valletta. There are similarities with St John's Co-Cathedral.

More difficult to find is the tiny church of Tal-Hlas, tucked away to the north of the town centre, worth seeking out for its barred iron windows in the façade. This useful feature protected the priest during pirate raids, while he said mass for his much less fortunate parishioners outside.

**Sidebar (Żabbar):**

29E3

7km southeast of Valletta

824383 (church museum)

Sun 9–12 (church museum)

Apart from a café (£) at the end of Santiwarju Street near the church, there is not much choice

18, 19, 21, 22, 23

Few

Free (church museum)

Marsaskala (➤ 51)

**Sidebar (Żebbuġ):**

28C3

8km southwest of Valletta

Nowhere suitable for a meal

88, 89

Few

ŻEJTUN ✪

Roman and Punic remains have been unearthed in Żejtun but the chief reason for visiting this old town, one of the 10 original parishes, lies with its two fine churches. On an island site the baroque church of St Catherine, a massively solid composition in stone, is regarded as the best example of Lorenzo Gafa's style. Some, though, may prefer the smaller church of St Gregory's, a few minutes walk away and close to the restful Luqa Briffa Gardens. St Grogory's, one of the best of the island's older churches, was medieval but in the 16th century the Knights made structural alterations and only the nave and façade remain faithful to the original. In 1969, secret wall passages revealed dozens of skeletons.

🚼 29E2
✉ 7km southeast of Valletta

St Catherine's Church
🕐 Mon–Fri 7–8AM; Sat 6:30–7:30; Sun 8–9AM, 11–noon
🍴 Café (£) is signposted from the square near St Catherine's
🚌 27, 28, 29, 30
♿ Few
↔ Tarxien Temples (➤ 26), Birżebbuġa (➤ 45), Marsaskala (➤ 51)

ŻURRIEQ ✪

This market town, one of the 10 original parishes, is usually just passed through *en route* to the Blue Grotto or Haġar Qim but there are two interesting churches. The exterior of the church of St Catherine is not exceptional but inside there are paintings by Mattia Preti, done by the artist when he fled here to escape a plague in 1675. Just 1km west of Żurrieq, off the road to the Blue Grotto, and in a deserted medieval settlement, is the delightful **Hal-Millieri Church of the Annunciation**. This chapel was built by farmers in 1420, abandoned in the 17th century, and rediscovered and renovated in the 1960s. The design is simple and the door is usually kept locked. Nevertheless the church has a wonderfully antique atmosphere and is utterly different in spirit to Malta's usual baroque ecclesiastical edifices.

🚼 29D2
✉ 9km south of Valletta

Hal-Millieri Church of Annunciation
☎ 220358 (National Trust, in charge of the Hal Millieri church)
🕐 First Sunday of each month 10–noon
🍴 Cafés and restaurants (£)
🚌 32, 33, 34
♿ Few

Shopping in Żebbuġ

Gozo

Gozo is only 14km long by 7km wide, one third the size of Malta, but the island is no mere adjunct. The prehistoric stones of Ġgantija testify to its long history, and the mighty citadel at Victoria demonstrates how important it was to both the Arabs and the Romans. Today, the island is grappling with the dilemma of encouraging its tourist industry while trying to preserve the traditional way of life that draws visitors here in the first place. The balance is still a healthy one.

There is only one sandy beach and no obvious resort areas, so visitors should not come expecting to find cosmopolitan distractions. The pace of life is slower in this agricultural and fishing community, which is the essence of Gozo's appeal. Fewer and smaller roads, less sense of congestion and a calmer atmosphere and superb swimming and diving, combine to produce a place of escape and relaxation.

*'Its coast scenery may
truly be called
pomskizillious and
gromphibberous, being
as no words can describe
its magnificence.'*

EDWARD LEAR
Letter to Lady Waldegrave (1866)

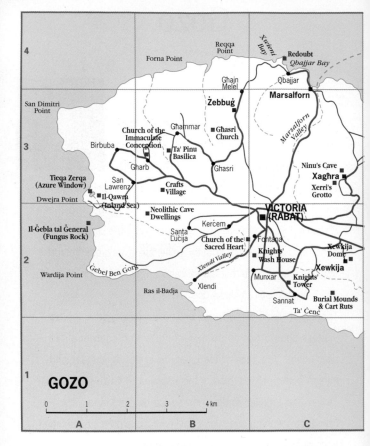

Map labels:

4 — Reqqa Point, Forna Point, Xwieni Bay, Redoubt, Qbajjar Bay, Ghajn Melel, Qbajjar, Żebbuġ, Marsalforn

San Dimitri Point

3 — Ghammar, Church of the Immaculate Conception, Ghasri Church, Marsalforn Valley, Birbuba, Ta' Pinu Basilica, Ghasri, Ninu's Cave, Gharb, Xaghra, Tieqa Zerqa (Azure Window), San Lawrenz, Crafts Village, Xerri's Grotto, Il-Qawra (Inland Sea), Dwejra Point, VICTORIA (RABAT)

2 — Il-Ġebla tal General (Fungus Rock), Neolithic Cave Dwellings, Kerċem, Santa Luċija, Church of the Sacred Heart, Fontana, Knights' Wash House, Xewkija Dome, Gebel Ben Gorg, Xlendi Valley, Xewkija, Wardija Point, Munxar, Knights' Tower, Ras il-Badja, Xlendi, Sannat, Burial Mounds & Cart Ruts, Ta' Ċenċ

1 — GOZO

0 1 2 3 4 km

A   B   C

Victoria (Rabat)

Gozo's capital was called simply Rabat ('the town') until 1897 when a British Governor changed the name at the time of Queen Victoria's Diamond Jubilee, but the old name also remains in use.

The hilltop Citadel (Il-Kastell) is the focus of most visitors' interest and has a cathedral and museums. Victoria itself is a pleasant little town with a church worth seeing and a central square that buzzes with life in the morning before falling asleep during the afternoon. The central square, It-Tokk ('the meeting place'), has some tiny bars where one may sit and watch the gentle routine of Gozitan life, while a mysterious maze of narrow little streets and alleyways radiate out from the square.

The domed church of St George dominates the skyline of Victoria (Rabat) in Gozo

What to See in Victoria (Rabat)

✚ 85B3

Folklore Museum, Archaeological Museum and Natural Science Museum:

🕐 16 Jun–30 Sep: Mon–Sat 8:30–6:30. 1 Oct–31 Mar: Mon–Sat 8:30–4:30. 1 Apr–15 Jun: Mon–Sat 8:30–6:30. Sunday open all year. Craft Centre Apr–Sep: Mon–Sat 7:30–6:45. Oct–Mar: 7:15–4:45

🍴 Cafés and restaurants (£–££) within walking distance.

♿ Few

💷 Cheap

↔ Gozo Cathedral (➤ 85)

Victoria Tourist Office

✉ 1 Palm Street, Victoria

☎ 558106

🕐 Mon–Sat 7:15–6, Sun 9–1

THE CITADEL ✪✪✪

The origins of this fortified enclave go back to Gozo's early history under Roman and Arab occupation. In 1551 Turkish raiders penetrated its defences and soon after this the Knights set about constructing sturdy bastions and ordering all Gozitans to spend their nights inside its walls – a policy that did not officially come to an end for almost 100 years. Now, the Citadel is virtually uninhabited at night, though by day there is a constant flow of travellers visiting the cathedral, the few craft shops and many museums.

The Cathedral Museum has church silver downstairs, ecclesiastical paintings upstairs and on the ground floor the bishop's 19th-century carriage last used in 1975. The **Folklore Museum** is the favourite of many visitors with its down-to-earth collection of practical artefacts, including two splendid mills. The **Archaeological Museum** has an important collection of Roman remains and Gozitan antiquities and, if time is limited, this and the Folklore Museum are the two worth seeing. An interesting exhibit is a 12th-century Arabic tombstone, inscribed in Kufic characters, mourning the premature death of a young Muslim girl. The **Natural Science Museum** has an unsurprising collection with the usual array of stuffed birds and geological exhibits. The **Armoury** is a disappointment because one can only peer through a gate at the exhibits. The Craft Centre has displays of local pottery, glass, wrought iron and lace which are not for sale but may whet your shopping appetite for the goods in some of the small craft shops inside the Citadel.

Many of the buildings inside the Citadel were destroyed by Dragut, in the seige of 1551, and in an earthquake of 1693, but the whole complex has been sympathetically restored and a walk around the ramparts offers terrific views while evoking a sense of Gozo's ancient past.

There are good views of Gozo from the Citadel's 400-year old walls, here looking east

GOZO CATHEDRAL ✪✪

The entrance to the Citadel in Victoria leads into a piazza with broad steps occupying most of one side, which lead up to the cathedral dedicated to the Assumption of Our Lady. The exterior is perfectly proportioned, as befits a building designed by Lorenzo Gafa, but there is no dome where Gafa intended one. Visual compensation is provided inside: the flat roof has the illusion of a dome painted onto it, this *trompe l'oeil* being an outstanding feature.

✚ 85B2
⊠ The Citadel
🕐 Mon–Sat 9–7, Sun for services
🍴 Cafés and restaurants (£–££) within walking distance
♿ Good
💲 Cheap
↔ The Citadel (➤ 84)

ST GEORGE'S CHURCH ✪✪

This lavishly decorated church, also known as the Basilica of St George, was built in 1678 after a design by Vittorio Cassar but with many alterations since, including a new façade in the 19th century and the addition of a dome and aisles in the 20th century. The interior is richly adorned, with a wealth of baroque trappings. The altar has alabaster decorated columns supporting a canopy, a diminutive copy of Bernini's in St Peter's in Rome. Some interesting art work includes a wooden statue of St George by Gozitan artist Paola Azzopardi that was carved from a single tree. The altarpiece is by Mattia Preti and the vault paintings are by Conti. The third Sunday in July celebrates the saint.

✚ 85B1
⊠ St George's Square
☎ 556377
🕐 Daily, 4:30AM–1PM, 3:30–7
🍴 Cafés and restaurants (£–££) within walking distance
♿ None
💲 Free
↔ The Citadel (➤ 84)

VICTORIA (RABAT)

85

What Else to See Around Gozo

THE AZURE WINDOW AND THE FUNGUS ROCK ✪✪

The natural phenomenon of *Il-Qawra* (Inland Sea) is a land-locked seawater pool but with a natural tunnel in the rock that allows the sea water in. A boat trip through the tunnel brings one to a door-like opening in the cliff through which one gazes at the Mediterranean. To Gozitans it has always been known as *Tieqa Zerqa* – the Azure Window – because of the colour of the dark blue sea. Nearby, off Dwejra Point, there is a rocky outcrop in the sea known as Fungus Rock.

➕ 82A3
✉ 2km west of San Lawrenz
🍴 Drinks and snacks (£) available in the car park area
🚌 91 from Victoria
♿ None
👐 Cheap

ĠGANTIJA TEMPLES (► 16, TOP TEN).

MARSALFORN ✪✪

The fishing village of Marsalforn was popular with those Gozitans who could afford a summer break long before it was discovered by tourists. It is the island's only resort area but a fairly low-key one compared with somewhere like St Julian's or St Paul's in Malta. There are waterside restaurants, bars and hotels, boat trips, and water activities can be arranged here. Bicycles can be hired in the village and, given the small size of Gozo, this opens up a lot of possibilities. A drawback to Marsalforn is that there is not much of a beach, but it is only a short walk to the nearby bays of Qbajjar and Xwejni and here visitors will have a bit more space.

➕ 82C4
✉ 4km north of Victoria
🍴 Cafés and restaurants (£–££) on the quayside
🚌 21 from Victoria
♿ Good

More of a door than a window, the Azure Window beckons to the blue expanse beyond

A Walk Around Gozo

For a walk in southern Gozo, drive or take a bus to Sannat, the most southerly village, and close to the Ta'Cenc cliffs.

At the southern end of Sannat follow both of the two signposted left turnings to Ta'Cenc/Dolmen/Cliffs.

It offers a fine view of Xewkija's domed church, The Rotunda (➤ 89) dominating the plain on your left.

You arrive at a roundabout of sorts (the roads are not surfaced) where you turn left, and not straight on which leads down to the sea and a small private beach belonging to the hotel.

The road you are on has a view of Comino and the western coastline of Malta up ahead in the distance, while all around is Gozo's barren landscape of limestone and scrubland. In this vicinity there are cart ruts (➤ 46) and Neolithic burial mounds, but they are not signposted and it takes a bit of luck to stumble across them.

After less than 1km the road acquires a surface and heads downhill for 600m; turn to the left just before the road becomes unsurfaced once more. The road you are now on is also unsurfaced and after about 0.5km the trail winds down to the inlet of Mġarr ix-Xini.

This is the perfect place for a rest and ideal for a picnic, and there is also the enticing prospect of a swim in the cool safe water.

From Mġarr ix-Xini it is 1.5km uphill along a surfaced road to a T-junction where the road to the right goes to Xewkija and the left road is signposted to Victoria. (Along this road to the left there is a bus stop and a service that will take you back to Victoria.)

Distance
4km

Time
2 hours

Start point
Sannat
✚ 82C2
🚌 50

End point
Just north of Mġarr ix-Xini
✚ 83D2
🚌 42,43

Lunch
Chip and Dale Bar (£)
✉ Town Square, Victoria
☎ 560506

Prickly pears in the foreground of the spectacular church at Xewkija

A relaxed enviable pace of a Gozitan passing the church in Sannat

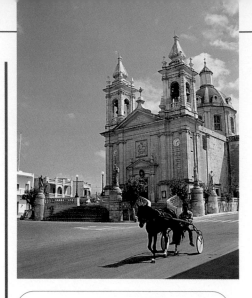

SANNAT

✪ 82C2
✉ 1.5km south of Victoria
🍴 Ta'Cenc Restaurant in the Ta'Cenc Hotel (££)
🚌 50 from Victoria
♿ Few
↔ Victoria (➤ 82–85)

The village of Sannat, just south of Victoria, has a reputation for lace-making and boasts a fine early 18th-century church, but the best reason for coming here is to begin a walk in the neighbouring plateau of Ta'Cenc. Gozo's top hotel (➤ 103) is also located in Ta'Cenc and to the east of it a track leads to the small harbour of Mġarr-ix-Xini. One could also walk west of Sannat to Xlendi via Munxar.

TA'PINU

✪ 82B3
✉ 2.5km northwest of Victoria
☎ 556992
🚌 61 from Victoria
♿ Few
❓ Multilingual information telephones are available

This imposing basilica, built in 1920 to 1931, hardly blends in with the surrounding countryside but it is an impressive sight nonetheless. There was a chapel on the site from the 16th century which was named after a Pinu Gauci who spent his time and money repairing it in the 1670s. At the end of the 19th century a local woman claimed to hear a voice in the church and gradually it acquired such a reputation for miracles that a bigger church was built around the original, which can be still seen inside behind the apse.

XAGHRA ✪ ✪

The area around this small town has a number of archaeological sites, the most famous of which is Ġgantija, but Xagħra is worth a visit in its own right. The delightful town square is home to the attractive Church of the Nativity and near by there is an old windmill still in working order. Also in Xagħra is a **Toy Museum**, and **Xerri's Grotto** in Gnien Imrik Street is also open to the public. The 2-km route from Xagħra to Calypso's Cave is well signposted but the trip is sadly disappointing because a dark hole in the cliff does not accord with anyone's idea of the site of Odysseus' seven-year abode with Calypso. What is worthwhile is the walk here from the east of Xagħra along a footpath through the lush Ramla valley.

XEWKIJA ✪ ✪

The people of this ancient village decided to build a larger church, now known as the Rotunda Church, and for the next 27 years money and labour from the villagers alone fed the construction of a massive edifice that is out of all proportion to the size of the village, and even to Gozo itself. The spectacular dome, which is only comparable to St Peter's in Rome and St Paul's in London, is 75m high and 28m in diameter.

XLENDI ✪

A forgotten little fishing village until tourism took hold of it, Xlendi is still a charming spot with a small beach that would be ideal if no one else came here. In the summer the promenade is full of souvenir and craft shops and there are a number of places facing the sea to stop for a drink or a meal. There is also a good hotel (▶ 103) making a longer stay possible.

✚ 82C3
✉ 3km east of Victoria
🍴 Café & bar (£) in town square but best to eat in Victoria
🚌 64, 65 from Victoria
↔ Ġgantija (▶ 16)

Toy Museum
☎ 562489
🕐 Mon–Sat 10–12, 3 6
👋 Cheap

Xerri's Grotto
☎ 560572
🕐 Daily 9–6 👋 Cheap

✚ 82C2
✉ 2km southeast of Victoria
🍴 Nearest restaurants are in Victoria
🚌 42 or 43 from Victoria
♿ Few

✚ 82B2
✉ 3km southwest of Victoria
🍴 Cafés and restaurants (£–££)
🚌 87 from Victoria
♿ Few
↔ Sannat (▶ 88)

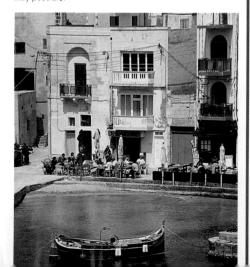

Fresh seafood, alfresco, at Xlendi in true Mediterranean fashion

A Drive Around Gozo

Distance
12km

Time
2–5 hours depending on visits

Start point
Mġarr ferry terminal
✠ 83D2

End point
Dwejra
✠ 82A3

Lunch
Il-Kartell (£–££)
✉ Waterfront in Marsalforn
☎ 556918

The northern coast of Gozo can be breezy and was once desolate – a place of legends.

After disembarking at Mġarr follow the signposted road to the right for Nadur. The uphill road leads to a T-junction; take the right turn for Qala, less than 1km away. Exposed Qala has remnants of windmills, sun-baked dwellings and dusty roads with a Moorish feel. Turn left at the main church, signposted for Nadur, and left again at the large unsignposted square with a religious statue in the centre.

At Nadur, an ancient look-out point, the church of Sts Peter and Paul may be visited for its painted ceiling and the skeletal relic of St Coronatus.

Leave Nadur on the road to Victoria and after 1.5km take the right turn at the roundabout for Xagħra. Follow the signs for Xagħra and follow the road as it climbs uphill with a sign on the right for Ġgantija (➤ 16). Stay on the road to Xagħra after Ġgantija but take the second turning on the right, passing down the side of the church and bearing left at the signposted junctions for Marsalforn.

There is a good view of Marsalforn as you enter the village through this backdoor approach. Stop here for lunch and a walk.

Take the road to Victoria from Marsalforn but turn right at the main junction before entering Victoria and look for the sign to Ta' Pinu (➤ 88).

The basilica at Ta'Pinu, a centre of pilgrimage for both Gozitans and Maltese, is noted for its mysterious voices and miraculous cures.

Statues outside the church of Ta'Pinu on the southern coast of Gozo

After the short detour to Ta'Pinu, return to the main road and take the signposted left turn for Dwejra. At St Lawrenz bear left in front of the church; the Azure Window is 1km (➤ 86).

Where To...

Malta

Prices
Approximate prices for a three-course meal for one without drinks and service:
£   = under LM5
££ = between LM5–10
£££ = above LM10

Fresh Bread
If you are up at around six in the morning you may hear the loud honking of the bread delivery van announcing its arrival in a street. The Maltese take their bread (*hobza*) seriously and in villages there are often two deliveries a day. Be sure to buy your loaf before 11AM in the morning.

Valletta and Floriana
Bologna Restaurant (££)
On a corner of Republic Street near Palace Square, this cosy little upstairs bar and Italian restaurant is a reliable middle-of-the-road restaurant. Pasta, meat and fish fill the menu and worth trying are the giant Mediterranean prawns grilled with lemon and parsley. At lunchtime the place can be busy but at night it often takes on a subdued and pleasantly discreet atmosphere.
✉ 59 Republic Street, Valletta
☎ 246149 🕐 Mon–Sat 12–2:15, 7–10:15

Café La Veneziana (£)
This small, airy café is a well-established and reliable eatery serving take-aways, breakfast, homemade burgers, salads and ice-cream.
✉ 29 Melita Street, Valletta
☎ 222513 🕐 Daily 7–10

Café Marquee (£)
There are tables inside, but only the weather keeps people away from the outdoor tables facing St John's Co-Cathedral. No surprises with the food: pizzas, burgers, pastas, salads, sandwiches and ice-cream.
✉ St John's Square, Valletta
☎ 236257 🕐 Daily 9–7

Café Premier (£)
The musty interior may be much as it was decades ago, although there are outdoor tables which are ideal for people-watching while enjoying a drink and a light lunch.
✉ Republic Square, Valletta
☎ 247300 🕐 Daily 9.30–5

The Carriage (£££)
Most fine dining establishments in Valletta are not easily found, but The Carriage is the exception to the rule. Its location is not superb but there are views of the cityscape. The decor is a soothing, cool white and blue and, while at lunchtime the local business fraternity dominates the scene, the weekend evenings are calmer. The food is a blend of various cuisines and should not disappoint; the starters are especially delicious.
✉ 22–5 Valletta Buildings, South Street, Valletta
☎ 247828 🕐 Mon–Thu 12–3:30, Fri–Sat 12–3:30, 8–10:45

Eddie's Café Regina (£)
The interior is brightly lit but the tables outside in Republic Square are even more brightly lit on a warm Mediterranean morning. Pizzas, pastas, grills, milkshakes and one or two Maltese dishes, including *qarabali* (stuffed marrows). Easily distinguished from the other cafés in the square by the green colour of the tables and waiters' uniforms.
✉ Republic Square, Valletta
☎ 246454 🕐 Daily 10–10

De Lucia (£)
An unpretentious little café, handy for the Museum of Fine Arts in the same street, serving excellent caper and bean salads, light snacks and good coffee. Newspapers available for reading.
✉ 28a South Street, Valletta
☎ 236258 🕐 Mon–Fri 8–8, Sat 8–1PM. Closed Sun

MLP Bar and Restaurant (£)
This affable little place is centrally located on the first floor of a Republic Street building. Plain tables and a

coin-operated snooker table adorn this informal meeting place for local people. The food is plain but there is plenty of it, and when the eat-all-you-can buffet is not operating there is a choice of pastas, steaks, grills, salads and fish. Breakfast is also served.

✉ **41 Republic Street, Valletta** ☎ **242592** ⊙ **Daily 7AM–midnight**

Perfection Café (£)

A dozen tables tucked away down Old Theatre Street serving light meals and snacks like burgers, toasted sandwiches, salads and some vegetarian choices. A take-away service is available, and after 6PM the evening meal menu is posted outside.

✉ **Old Theatre Street, Valletta** ☎ **237992** ⊙ **Mon–Fri 8–8, Sat 8–1:30PM, 5–9**

Phoenix Restaurant (£££)

Given the prestige of the Phoenicia Hotel, its flagship restaurant has a lot to live up to, but it emerges with flying, albeit expensive, colours. The cuisine is inventive and innovative and reading the menu will whet most appetites as one contemplates, for example, poached dumplings of duck, pistachios and wild mushrooms with avocado, truffles and cream.

✉ **Phoenicia Hotel, The Mall, Floriana** ☎ **225241** ⊙ **Daily 12:30–2:30, 7–10:30**

Restorante de Vilhena (£)

A delightful location in a small covered courtyard next to the Manoel Theatre. The restaurant only serves evening meals when there is a performance in the theatre. The small menu consists of mainly pasta dishes.

✉ **115 Old Theatre Street, Valletta** ☎ **232574** ⊙ **Mon–Fri 9–3PM. Also at weekends when there is a play showing.**

Scalini (££)

A small Italian menu with mostly meat dishes, for example *scalloppini ai funghi*. The interior is pleasantly cool and unpretentious.

✉ **South Street (opposite the Museum of Fine Arts), Valletta** ☎ **246221** ⊙ **Mon–Fri 12–2:30, 7–11, Sat 7–11**

Seventh Heaven Restaurant (£)

Try to reserve a window table for the arresting view from a hotel restaurant that is perched on a bastion of Valletta, overlooking Vittoriosa and the Grand Harbour. The food is quite interesting with some vegetarian possibilities like stuffed aubergines as well as meat dishes.

✉ **Grand Harbour Hotel, 47 Battery Street, Valletta** ☎ **246003** ⊙ **Daily 12–2, 7–10**

Around Malta

Balzan

Corinthia Room Restaurant (£££)

The main restaurant of the Corinthia Palace Hotel and one of the best in Malta. The setting is superb. There is one central dining area with the surrounding rooms of the villa forming dining adjuncts. The whole place is elegantly furnished and decorated in a grand style. European menu.

✉ **Corinthia Palace Hotel, De Paule Avenue, Attard** ☎ **440301** ⊙ **Daily 12:30–2:30, 6:30–10** 🚌 **40**

Il–Melita (£)

There are two entrances to San Anton Gardens (➤ 44) and the Il-Melita bar and pizzeria is situated next to the one on Birkirkara Street. Not a touristy restaurant but it is a good place for a drink and meal after visiting the Gardens.

✉ **Birkirkara Street, San Anton Gardens, Balzan** ☎ **441073** ⊙ **Tue–Sun 12–2:30, 5–11; Mon 5–11** 🚌 **40**

A Fish Dictionary

MALTESE	ENGLISH
acciola	amberjack
cerna	grouper
dorado	swordfish
dott	stone bass
klamer	squid
pagru	sea bream
san pietro	john dory
pesce sicca	cuttlefish

Pastizzi
The traditional Maltese snack is sometimes translated as cheesecake but this can be misleading. They are in fact made from a rich flaky pastry and a savoury filling of ricotta cheese or dried peas. They are eaten mid-morning or mid-afternoon with a tea or coffee. High in calories but friendly to the taste buds.

Rickshaw Restaurant (££)
This hotel restaurant serves an inventive miscellany of oriental dishes from India, Thailand, Malaysia and China. Meat and seafood predominate and none of the dishes are spicy. Before or after a meal enjoy a drink in the Caprice Lounge, which is open until the early hours of the morning and has live music.
✉ **Corinthia Palace Hotel, De Paule Avenue, Balzan**
☎ **440301** ⏰ **Mon–Sat 6PM–11**
🚌 **40**

Dingli Cliffs
Bobbyland Bar and Restaurant (£)
A landmark restaurant which is not easily missed if you turn to the right after arriving at Dingli Cliffs from Rabat. At weekends in the summer the tables are oversubscribed and there can be an air of frenzy about the place. Come at a quieter time and the view out to sea will overwhelm. The food is usually excellent, with an emphasis on traditional meat dishes featuring rabbit and lamb, but the fish is always a welcome alternative.
✉ **Dingli Cliffs** ☎ **452895**
⏰ **Tue–Fri 11:30–2:30, 7–10:30, Sat 11:30–2, 7–10:30, Sun 11:30–2:15, 7–10** 🚌 **81**

Marsaskala
Al Kafe (£)
A pleasant *pizzeria* and cafeteria with a prime location on the waterfront and tables filling the pavement under giant umbrellas. There is a pub a few doors down, Summer Nights, under the same management and there is also a guest house.
✉ **Marina Street, Marsaskala**
☎ **632528** ⏰ **Wed–Mon 8AM–11PM** 🚌 **19, 22**

Beluga (£–££)
This seafood restaurant is popular with local people as well as visitors. The decor is smart, if a little sombre, and the fresh fish can always be relied on. The restaurant is located on a corner in the centre of Marsaskala.
✉ **Triq tal–Gardiel** ☎ **639452**
⏰ **Thu–Tue 6:30PM–11**
🚌 **19, 22**

Grabiel (££)
Probably the most popular restaurant with local people and deservedly so because the prices are reasonable and the food is very good. There is a wide range of starters and while the main dishes are mostly meat the counter is usually overflowing with examples of the locally caught fresh fish. The restaurant is right in the centre of town. Recommended.
✉ **Mifsud Bonnici Square**
☎ **684194** ⏰ **Tue–Sat noon–2, 7–10:30, Sun noon–2PM. Closed in August** 🚌 **19, 22**

Jakarta (££)
This waterside restaurant has a small but smart interior with white linen tablecloths and a menu of oriental dishes. There is a set meal for two people besides the à la carte choices which include satay, spare-ribs and crispy duck with pancakes.
✉ **Pjazza Dun Tarcis Agius**
☎ **633993** ⏰ **Tue–Sun 7–11, Sun noon–2PM** 🚌 **19**

La Playa (£)
Waterfront location with wide menu of pastas, pizzas and salads and child-friendly items like chicken nuggets. Some pasta specialities like *farfalle moscovita* (cream with prawns, salmon, caviar and white fish).
✉ **Marsaskala waterfront**
☎ **616435** ⏰ **Tue–Sun 9:30–2:30, 6–midnight,** 🚌 **19, 20**

Tudor Inn (££)
English-style decor adorns this very pleasant, family-run restaurant that specialises in

fish and Italian food. The fresh fish is displayed by the door and there are also appetising seafood starters like *piatto misto* (mixed shellfish). This cosy little restaurant is located on the quieter seafront side in Marsaskala.

✉ 68 Salina Street, Marsaskala
☎ 684139 ◷ Thu–Tue 7pm–10:30, Sun noon–2PM
🚌 19, 20, 22

Marsaxlokk
Ir-Rizzu (££)

This is an excellent fish restaurant and it is easily found on the sea front in Marsaxlokk. Meat dishes are available but locals wax lyrical about the variety of fish available and the unerring skill with which it is prepared for the table. This is partly because the traditional Maltese method of steaming fish is used here.

✉ Xatt is-Sjjieda ☎ 871569
◷ Daily 12–2:30, 7–10 🚌 27 from Valletta, 427 from Buġibba, 627 from Paceville

Mdina and Rabat
Bacchus (££)

The bare stone walls of this restaurant once housed Mdina's store of gunpowder but, notwithstanding a dungeon-like atmosphere, this is one of the best places for a decent meal in Mdina. There are some tasty *hors d'oeuvres* served with side dishes of vegetable or salad, speciality fish dishes, soups, grills and pasta.

✉ Inguanez Street, Mdina
☎ 454981 ◷ Daily 10–midnight 🚌 80, 81 from Valletta, 65 from Sliema

Caffé Medina (£)

Like many of the restaurants in Mdina, Caffé Medina closes early in the evening, but unlike the others it keeps later hours at the weekend. The menu, however, is a fairly insubstantial one, just salads, toasted sandwiches

and special ice-creams.

✉ 9 Triq Villegaignon, Mdina
☎ 451917 ◷ Mon–Thu 9:30–6, Fri–Sat 9:30–11, Sun 9:30–7
🚌 80, 84 from Valletta, 65 from Sliema

Ciappetti (£)

Lovely courtyard setting with wooden tables and a simple short menu of salads, rolls and home-made cakes. There is an open-air terrace upstairs on the bastion.

✉ 5 St Agatha's Esplanade, Mdina ☎ 459987 ◷ Daily 10–6 🚌 80, 81 from Valletta, 65 from Sliema

La Citta Vecchia (£)

Superb location with a tea room and small shop downstairs, and terrace seating upstairs with fine views. The speciality here is very good value, a filling ploughman's lunch that includes a glass of wine. Recommended.

✉ Bastion Square, Mdina
☎ 454511 ◷ Mon–Fri 10–4, Sat 10–2 🚌 80, 81 from Valletta, 65 from Sliema

Cuckoo's Nest Tavern (£)

This is one of the tiniest restaurants in Malta with three tables and a diminutive bar, but it has character. The food is nearly all meat dishes featuring beef and lamb.

✉ 9 St Paul Street, Rabat
☎ 455946 ◷ Daily 11:30–2:30, 7–10 🚌 80, 81, 83, 84 from Valletta, 65 from Sliema, 86 from Buġibba

Fontanella (£)

Panoramic view from the tables of the battlements of Mdina. Only light meals like sandwiches and salads but excellent selection of home-made cakes – lemon meringue, black forest gateau. Recommended.

✉ 1 Bastion Street, Mdina
☎ 454264 ◷ Summer: daily 10–10. Winter 10–6 🚌 80, 81 from Valletta, 65 from Sliema

Fenek biz–zalza

Rabbit has been eaten in Malta for as long as anyone can remember and in rabbit stew (*fenek biz–zalza*) the taste has been perfected. The rabbit is fried in a mixture of red wine and fat and then stewed slowly with vegetables, herbs and more wine. Sometimes the rabbit is roasted or served inside a pie along with vegetables and pieces of pork – *torta tal-fenek*.

Sweet Deserts

The British influence may account for the puddings but Italy must be thanked for the *gelaterias* (ice-cream parlours) and Sicily is regarded as the source of *kannoli*, a dessert that is worth seeking out. It comprises cornets of deep–fried pastry filled with ricotta cheese and sweetened with chocolate.

A Maltese Picnic
Glorious weather invites a picnic so prepare *hobz biz–zejt* (bread with oil) or purchase it at a coffee shop. Traditionally the farmer's packed lunch, thick bread is dipped in olive oil then spread with pulped tomato before being heaped with olives, capers, garlic, vinegar and salt and pepper.

Grapes (£)
An inexpensive and colourful place to rest and eat after visiting the catacombs. The special dishes are traditional Maltese ones, washed down with home-made wine.

✉ 1 Catacombs Street, Rabat
☎ 450483 🕐 Mon–Fri 11–3, 6:30–10, Sat 11–3, 6:30–11 🚌 80, 81, 83, 84 from Valletta, 65 from Sliema, 86 from Buġibba

Peristyle Restaurant and Bar (£–££)
This restaurant offers a reasonable range of pizzas, *à la carte* meals and local wines. In tune with its location opposite Rabat's Roman villa, the restaurant attempts a classical decor. It is under the same management as the Stazzjon Restaurant (► right).

✉ Opposite Museum of Roman Antiquities, Rabat ☎ 451717
🕐 Daily 9AM–midnight 🚌 80, 81, 83, 84 from Valletta, 65 from Sliema, 86 from Buġibba

Point de Vue (£–££)
Located just outside Mdina Gate, this is a tourist restaurant with menus in English, French and German. There are outdoor and inside tables and some of the Maltese dishes make a refreshing change. (The French and German menus carry more Maltese meals than the English one – a management decision no doubt based on experience) Try the *haruf imsajjar fl-imbio* (spicy marinated lamb in wine) which appears on all the menus. There are also inexpensive set meals.

✉ 5 The Saqqajja, Rabat
☎ 454117 🕐 Daily 9–11:30 🚌 80, 81, 83, 84 from Valletta, 65 from Sliema, 86 from Buġibba

Ristorante Gusmana Navarra (££)
Rabat's restaurants like to harmonise with their surroundings, and this one opposite St Paul's Church has a fairly large religious grotto next to one of the tables in the downstairs bar area, which also serves snacks. The restaurant upstairs serves meat and some fish dishes; also an inexpensive set menu.

✉ 28 St Paul's Street, Rabat
☎ 450638 🕐 Mon–Sat 6:30–10 (bar open daily 4–midnight). Closed Sun 🚌 80, 81, 83, 84 from Valletta, 65 from Sliema, 86 from Buġibba

Stazzjon Restaurant (££)
This restaurant does not let you forget its unique setting in the last station on the steam–train route which ran from Valletta until 1931. Drinks are ordered at the ticket window and the dining area occupies what was the waiting room as well as the platform. The *à la carte* menu offers pasta, grills and fish and the prices are reasonable. It is a ten-minute walk from the Museum of Roman Antiquities.

✉ Mtarfa Road, Rabat
☎ 451717 🕐 Tue–Sun 7PM–1AM 🚌 80, 83, 84 from Valletta, 65 from Sliema, 86 from Buġibba

Mellieha
Alantil Bay Restaurant (£)
This family-run bar and restaurant serves snacks, grills, salads and burgers. No surprises with the food except for a couple of Maltese dishes like rabbit and *bragioli* (rolled sliced beef filled with ham), but it is inexpensive and reliable and there are outside tables.

✉ 61 Dr G Borg Oliver Street, Mellieha ☎ 573049 🕐 Daily 10–1PM 🚌 43, 44, 45 from Valletta, 48 from Buġibba and Ċirkewwa, 645 from Sliema and Ċirkewwa

The Arches (£££)
Centrally located on the main street, The Arches restaurant has long been considered

one of the best in Malta. It has a good wine list and the European cuisine is complemented by mouth-watering desserts. The dining area seats 90 so it can become noisy, but the quality of the food is the best distraction.

✉ 113 Borg Oliver Street
☎ 573436 ⏰ Mon–Sat 7–10:30
🚌 43, 44, 45 from Valletta, 48 from Buġibba and Ċirkewwa, 645 from Sliema and Ċirkewwa

Billy's Restaurant (££)
Entering Mellieha from the south, Billy's hotel, bar and restaurant is on the right before going down the hill. There is a large menu of meat dishes plus pasta and fish. Children are welcome and there is a games room.
✉ Main Street ☎ 523049
⏰ Daily 6:30–11 🚌 43, 44, 45 from Valletta, 48 from Buġibba and Ċirkewwa, 645 from Sliema and Ċirkewwa

Il-Mulino (££)
Authentic Italian food at this pretty restaurant. The downstairs indoor section is pleasant while upstairs there is a terrace. Recommended.
✉ 45 Main Street, Mellieha
☎ 520404 ⏰ Summer: Tue–Sun 7–11. Winter: Tue–Sat 6:30–10:30, Sun 11:30–3PM
🚌 43, 44, 45 from Valletta, 48 from Buġibba and Ċirkewwa, 645 from Sliema and Ċirkewwa

Mġarr
Charles il–Barri (£–££)
There are not many restaurants in the area so this establishment serves a useful purpose when visiting nearby places of interest. There are inexpensive pizzas as well as substantial dishes. The bar keeps longer and later hours.
✉ Next to the church in the town square, Jubilee Esplanade
☎ 573235 ⏰ Restaurant: Tue–Sat 12–2:30, 7–10. Bar: 9–3:30, 5:15–midnight
🚌 47

St Julian's, Paceville and St George's Bay
Barracuda ££)
The original beams of an 18th-century residence still support this waterfront restaurant. The food is Italian but the speciality is always the fresh fish, cooked whole.
✉ 194 Main Street, St Julian's
☎ 331817 ⏰ 7–10:30. Closed Sun in the winter 🚌 62, 64, 67, 68, 70 from Valletta, 627 between Paceville and Marsaxlokk

Caffe Raffael (£)
Pizza, pasta, salads and kebabs in a lovely stone–built restaurant. Reserve an outdoor waterfront table. Deservedly busy.
✉ St George's Road ☎ 319988
⏰ Daily 10–11 🚌 62, 64, 65, 67, 68, 70

La Dolce Vita (££–£££)
Holds its own as one of the best fish restaurants. Reserve a terrace table.
✉ 156 St George's Road
☎ 337806 ⏰ Daily 12–2:30, 7–11. Closed for lunch in winter
🚌 62, 64, 67, 68, 70 from Valletta, 627 between Paceville and Marsaxlokk

Fra Martino (££–£££)
This large place with over 200 seats inside and 150 outdoors still manages to evoke a very Mediterranean atmosphere. At night a pianist plays.
✉ San Gorg Corinthia Hotel, St George's Bay ☎ 374114
⏰ Daily 12:30–2, 7–11 🚌 62, 64, 65, 67, 68, 70

La Maltija (££)
The best for Maltese food, with suitably rustic decor. Starters include *aljotta* (fish soup) and spaghetti with rabbit sauce. Mains include *bragioli* (rolled sliced beef with ham), stuffed marrows and swordfish.
✉ 1 Church Street, Paceville
☎ 339602 ⏰ Mon–Sat 6–11, Sun 11–3, 6–11 🚌 62, 64, 65, 67

Delicious and Different
Look for *bigilla*, a dish served with toasted bread that originated during the privations of World War II when there was little choice of food. Mashed beans are mixed with a pumpkin sauce to make this delicious repast. Cumin and garlic give it a spicy taste. Served at the Barracuda in St Julian's (▶ left).

A Cheese with Attitude
Imported cheeses from Italy are readily available but it would be a pity to miss out on *gbejna*. This cheese made from goat's milk is now made in Malta but it is best enjoyed in Gozo from where it originates. The peppered version (*tal-bzar*) is far tastier than the unpeppered.

Marquis Room (££)
If you want to visit The Casino (➤ 110), with or without the chance of a flutter, its restaurant is a perfect excuse. Dark wood and dim lighting characterise the interior. The steaks are famously good but for a non–meat dish try the king prawns flamed with cognac and Pernod. Some tables are by the window looking into the casino. A jacket and tie are required.
✉ The Casino, Dragonara Point, St Julian's ☎ 344550
🕐 Tue–Sun 8:30–midnight
🚌 62, 64, 65, 67, 68, 70

Paparazzi (£–££)
Out of the cluster of restaurants in the Spinola Bay area, Paparazzi offers value for money. Individually cooked pizzas and pasta dishes take 15 to 20 minutes to arrive on your table, time waiting easily passed if sitting outside overlooking the sea.
✉ 159 St George's Road
☎ 374965 🕐 Daily 5–midnight
🚌 62, 64, 65, 67, 68, 70

Peppino's (££–£££)
At lunch time only the wine bar area is open for pasta and salads, but during the evening the top two floors have tables overlooking the bay and reservations are essential at weekends, especially for the top terrace which has a superb view. There is a good wine list.
✉ 31 St Georges Road, St Julian's ☎ 373200
🕐 Mon–Sat 12–2:30, 7–11
🚌 62, 64, 65, 67, 68, 70

St Paul's Bay and Buġibba
Beverley's Tavern (££)
The menu of Maltese dishes includes fairly detailed explanations of the various choices and there is also a Lebanese element to the cuisine (the proprietor is Lebanese). A speciality is rabbit stew and there is a *spaghetti biz–zalza tal-Fenek* (spaghetti with rabbit sauce) starter.
✉ Pioneer Road, Buġibba
☎ 571350 🕐 Daily 9–2AM
🚌 49 from Valletta, 48 from Ċirkewwa, 51 from Għajn Tuffieħa, 70, 645, 652, from Sliema, 86 between Buġibba and Rabat, 427 between Buġibba and Marsaxlokk

Gillieru Restaurant (££–£££)
A well–established and renowned restaurant with a seafront location; reserve one of the outside tables. The menu is mainly seafood and the freshly caught fish is also used for Maltese dishes like *klamar mimli* (stuffed squid with egg, olives, anchovies and tomatoes). A 15 per cent discount for hotel residents.
✉ 66 Church Street, St Paul's Bay ☎ 573480 🕐 Daily 12:15–2:30, 7:30–11 (bar open 10AM–midnight) 🚌 43, 44, 45, 49, 50 from Valletta, 48 from Ċirkewwa

Macedonia (£)
Three eating places here: a Chinese upstairs, a *pizzeria* downstairs and a café/bar on the middle level. The *pizzeria* has a good reputation and is often crowded at weekends.
✉ 47 Church Street, St Paul's Bay ☎ 573391 🕐 Daily 7PM–midnight 🚌 43, 44, 45, 49, 50 from Valletta, 48 from Ċirkewwa

Nettuno (£–££)
Steaks, rabbit, fish, octopus stew and inexpensive pizzas. The place lacks character but the food is enjoyed by Maltese as well as visitors. It is on the left approaching the Mistra Village complex from St Paul's.
✉ Xemxija Hill, St Paul's Bay
☎ 573818 🕐 Daily 9–2AM
🚌 43, 44, 45, 49, 50 from Valletta, 48 from Ċirkewwa

Sliema

L'Aristocrat (££–£££)
Comfortable with a relaxed atmosphere; the European food is very good.

✉ Diplomat Hotel, 173 Tower Road, Sliema ☎ 345361
🕐 Mon–Sat 7–11 🚌 60, 61, 62, 63, 64, 67, 68 from Valletta, 70 from Buġibba, 65 from Rabat, 86 from Buġibba, 645 from Ċirkewwa, 652 from Golden Bay

Four Seasons Restaurant (£££)
A formally elegant restaurant with white linen tablecloths and a restrained atmosphere. An excellent range of antipasti, a good choice of fish, fine cheeses and a good wine list.

✉ Holiday Inn Crowne Plaza, Tigne Street, Sliema ☎ 341173
🕐 Daily 11–11 🚌 60, 61, 62, 63, 64, 67, 68 from Valletta, 70 from Buġibba, 65 from Rabat, 86 from Buġibba and Rabat, 645 from Ċirkewwa, 652 from Golden Bay

Vittoriosa

The Old City Pub (£)
Vittoriosa has little to offer by way of restaurants or even cafés, but the Old City Pub can offer fine views from the quayside. The menu is the usual range of quickly prepared light meals. The closing hours are useful after a late night stroll.

✉ Quayside, Vittoriosa
☎ 663614 🕐 Daily 8–3, 6:30–midnight 🚌 1, 2, 4, 6

Gozo

Chip and Dale Bar (£)
A few outdoor tables where one can enjoy a drink and a light meal. Food is confined to giant rolls and toast.

✉ St Francis Square, Victoria
☎ 560506 🕐 Daily 7–11.30. Closed 2–4 🚌 25 from Mġarr ferry port

Cittadella Centre (££)
It has an indoor and outdoor dining area as well as a bar, cafeteria and ice-cream parlour. The pleasant decor is marred only by the plastic tables.

✉ 14 Sir Adrian Dingli Street
☎ 556628 🕐 12–3, 7–11
🚌 25 from Mġarr ferry port

Fuhuq Restaurant (££)
On the road out of town to Victoria. It serves fairly innocuous oriental cuisine. The set meals are good value.

✉ Tritons Lodge, Rabat Road, Marsalforn ☎ 556152
🕐 Mon–Sat 6:30–midnight, Sun 12–2:30, 6:30–midnight 🚌 21 from Victoria

Jeffrey's (££)
A modest and friendly restaurant, with a small open air section at the back. The food is delicious, and while the menu follows what is locally available at the time, visitors may depend on fish, rabbit and pasta.

✉ 10 Triq l–Gharb ☎ 561006
🕐 Mon–Sat 7–11 🚌 2, 91 from Victoria

Il–Kartell (£–££)
A lively waterside restaurant with a good reputation for fresh fish. There is a helpful explanation on a notice board of the various types of local fish. A speciality is mixed seafood with cream, but pizzas are also available. Music at night.

✉ Marsalforn Bay ☎ 556918
🕐 Summer: daily noon–4, 6–midnight. Winter: Fri–Sun only. 🚌 21 from Victoria

Ta'Cenc Hotel Restaurant (£££)
Reserve a table, preferably under the ancient carob tree, to soak up the atmosphere while tucking into local fish. There are some tasty Italian alternatives to fish. Recommended.

✉ Hotel Ta'Cenc, Sannat
☎ 561522 🕐 Daily 1–2:30, 7:30–9:30 🚌 50 from Victoria

Stuffed Delights
Stuffed dishes are common in Maltese cuisine. Octopus, squid and cuttlefish are all stuffed, as are aubergines, marrows and peppers. Vegetarians should ask for stuffed vegetables without mincemeat for this is often added to the onions, tomatoes, herbs and breadcrumbs that make up the filling.

Malta

Prices

Expect to pay for a room per night –

£	= under LM10
££	= LM10–40
£££	= over LM40

Valletta and Floriana

British Hotel (£–££)

The longest established hotel in Valletta has a lovely situation overlooking the Grand Harbour. All 44 rooms on six floors have *en suite* facilities and telephone, and some have balconies. A rooftop sundeck for sun bathing and drinks and an inexpensive restaurant compensate for the narrow corridors and stairs.

✉ **267 St Ursula Street, Valletta** ☎ **224730**

Forte Grand Phoenicia (£££)

The prestigious Phoenicia carries its distinction with great *élan*. Built in the 1920s, it was carefully modernised in the 1990s to preserve its classical grandeur. The rooms are furnished and decorated in an enviable style of simple elegance with understated touches of luxury. There are bars, restaurants, fitness room, pool and terraced gardens.

✉ **The Mall, Floriana** ☎ **225241**

Grand Harbour Hotel (£)

A superb location with outstanding views of the Grand Harbour and an inexpensive restaurant. The rooms can be small and facilities are basic but nevertheless this still represents value for money.

✉ **47 Battery Street, Valletta** ☎ **246003**

Around Malta

Balzan

Corinthia Palace Hotel (£££)

One of the top hotels in Malta. The rooms have everything from fax points to hair dryers and the hotel's health spa is state-of-the-art with sauna, massage, gym, mudstream baths, aromatheraphy and reflexology. Indoor and outdoor pools and tennis and squash courts complete the fitness facilities. There is also a courtesy bus to Valletta.

✉ **De Paule Av, Balzan** ☎ **440301** 🚌 **40**

Comino

Comino Hotel (£££)

If staying on Comino you'll be residing here, the only hotel on the island. There are nearly 150 rooms with either balconies or gardens, and while many people come to Comino for peaceful relaxation, the hotel has an impressive array of sports facilities. There are also two private beaches and a disco at night.

✉ **Comino** ☎ **529821** 🚢 **Hotel operates its own ferry service from Čirkewwa and Mġarr**

Marsaskala

Jerma Palace Hotel (£££)

A 15–minute walk from Marsaskala village, this is easily the best hotel in the area. Most of the 350 rooms have sea views, and facilities include an indoor heated pool, an outdoor seawater pool, children's pools and a pool bar. Watersports can be arranged and there is a good restaurant.

✉ **Marsaskala** ☎ **633222** 🚌 **19, 20, 22**

Mdina and Rabat

Point de Vue (£)

This family-run budget guesthouse is in a 17th-century building and apparently guests have been staying here since 1898. The location is central, just outside Mdina Gate, and some of the rooms can offer a balcony as well as picturesque views of the surrounding Maltese countryside.

✉ 5 The Saqqajja, Rabat
☎ 454117 🚌 80, 81, 83, 84, 86, 65

Mellieha
Maritim Selmun Palace (£££)

Just outside Mellieha, this grand hotel stands on a hill overlooking the sea. There are rocky beaches within walking distance and a sandy stretch which is operated by the hotel. There are also indoor and outdoor pools and a sauna. The hotel is partly owned by a German company and as well as speaking German the staff of the Maritim Selmun Palace can communicate in English, French, Italian and Dutch.

✉ Selmun, Mellieha
☎ 521040 🚌 43, 44, 45 from Valletta, 48 from Buġibba and Ċirkewwa, 645 from Sliema and Ċirkewwa

Mellieha Holiday Centre (££)

This Danish-run complex comprises 150 self-catering bungalows, each with two bedrooms, Olympic-sized swimming pool, restaurant, bar, playground and supermarket. The bungalow tariff is reasonable and in winter enters the budget category.

✉ Mellieha Bay ☎ 573900
🚌 43

St Julian's, Paceville and St George's Bay
Eden Beach Hotel (££–£££)

Hotels do not come with many more facilities than those available here: restaurant, bar, coffee shop, water sports, tennis and squash courts, gym, sauna, beauty parlour, disco, and facilities for visitors with disabilities. The outdoor pool is heated in winter but there is also an indoor pool for adults. The children have their own pool.

✉ St George's Bay, St Julian's ☎ 341191
🚌 62, 64, 65, 67, 68, 70

Hotel Club Villa Rosa (£)

This brightly coloured hotel seems quite homely compared to the new giant hotel blocks that are gradually dominating the area. For a lot less money than those, the Villa Rosa offers indoor and outdoor pools, sports, gym and restaurant and easy access to nearby restaurants and also to the dynamic nightlife of Paceville.

✉ St George's Bay, St Julian's ☎ 342707
🚌 62, 64, 65, 67, 68, 70

Hotel San Gorg (£)

Rooms have *en suite* showers, 24-hour reception desk, bar, restaurant and the hotel is located in the heart of Paceville. This is not a quiet retreat, but if you want to be close to pubs and discos the Hotel San Gorg is good value for money.

✉ Ball Street, Paceville, St Julian's ☎ 336136 🚌 62, 64, 65, 67, 68, 70

St George's Park Complex (££)

With over 800 beds, there is quite a range of rooms, studios and apartments. During the winter, groups stay here for as long as three months at a time. The hotel's lido has two pools and there is a good leisure centre with squash courts, sauna and gym. The huge restaurant seats some 400 guests and there is also a pub.

✉ St George's Park, St Julian's ☎ 311782
🚌 62, 64, 65, 67, 68, 70

On the Move

Budget–conscious visitors to Malta and Gozo who plan to travel around the islands staying in different hotels and guest houses each night should collect from the tourist office a useful little brochure that lists all one- and two-star hotels, hostels and guest houses and explains the available facilites.

Staying Put

Visitors whose stay in Malta does not exceed three months are classified as non-residents. Anyone wishing to stay longer is required to show proof that their income will enable them to live independently in Malta. Temporary residents become subject to local taxes after six months.

San Gorg Corinthia (£££)

The St George's Bay area is being developed as an accommodation centre and the San Gorg holds pride of place. All 250 rooms on the six floors have a balcony and sea view. The water facilities are first class and there are health and fitness facilities. A sister hotel is planned for next door.

✉ St George's Bay, St Julian's
☎ 374114 🚌 62, 64, 65, 67, 68, 70

St Paul's Bay, Buġibba and Qawra

Blue Lagoon Hotel (£)

All the rooms have bathrooms *en suite*; 24-hour reception, bar and open-air restaurant.

✉ Mazzola Street, Buġibba
☎ 583748 🚌 49 from Valletta, 48 from Ċirkewwa, 51 from Għajn Tuffieħa, 70, 645, 652, from Sliema, 86 between Buġibba and Rabat, 427 between Buġibba and Marsaxlokk

Gillieru Harbour Hotel (££)

Located on the water's edge overlooking St Paul's Bay. All the rooms have bathrooms *en suite*, air-conditioning, balcony and satellite television. Also a swimming pool and restaurant.

✉ Church Square, St Paul's Bay ☎ 572716 🚌 43, 44, 45, 49, 50 from Valletta, 48 from Ċirkewwa

Mistra Village (£££)

This is a self-catering 'tourist village', ideal for families, especially those with young children. Well-organised, well-equipped apartments and a host of facilities and activities; tennis court, squash courts, fitness centre, sauna and pools; children have their own pools, play area, theatre and organised activities.

✉ Xemxija Hill, St Paul's Bay
☎ 580481 🚌 43, 44, 45, 50, 51, 52

New Dolmen Hotel (£££)

One of the largest hotels in Malta boasts an impressive array of facilities. Apart from the 387 bedrooms there are four outdoor pools, and one indoor one, a watersports centre, cocktail bar, leisure centre, two restaurants and a disco. Good facilities for visitors with disabilities.

✉ Qawra, St Paul's Bay
☎ 581510 🚌 48, 49, 51, 70, 86

Suncrest Hotel (£££)

With over 400 rooms, it manages to avoid being impersonal and it has the best facilities of any hotel in the area. There are five restaurants, a disco, two lidos and two outdoor pools, tennis and squash courts, a health centre and a water sports centre. Facilities for people with disabilites are very good.

✉ Qawra Coast Road, Qawra
☎ 577101 🚌 48, 49, 51, 70, 86

Xemxija Bay Hotel (£)

This is good value. All 21 rooms have air-conditioning, there is a small supplement for a room overlooking the sea and half-board is available at an economical price. The main road location means a 10-to 15-minute walk to St Paul's and Buġibba. Bus stop nearby.

✉ Xemxija, St Paul's Bay
☎ 573454 🚌 43, 44, 45, 50, 51

Sliema

Diplomat Hotel (££)

A well-run hotel for smart rooms and service. Residents are within walking distance of the promenade but this has a quieter seafront location. Find a rooftop pool, a restaurant, a 24-hour café and a cocktail bar with piano.

✉ Tower Road, Sliema
☎ 34536 🚌 60, 61, 62, 63, 64, 67, 68 from Valletta, 70 from Buġibba, 65 from Rabat, 86 from Buġibba and Rabat

Holiday Inn Crowne Plaza (£££)

This very modern hotel was built on the site of an 18th-century Knight's fort. There is an outdoor and heated indoor pool, gym with sauna and squash and tennis courts, and rooms have sea views or, less expensive, city views.

✉ **Tigne Street, Sliema**
☎ **341173** 🚌 **60, 61, 62, 63, 64, 67, 68 from Valletta, 70 from Buġibba, 65 from Rabat, 86 from Buġibba and Rabat. 645 from Ċirkewwa, 652 from Golden Bay**

Marina Hotel (££)

Overlooking the Tigne seafront in Sliema, pay the supplement for a sea view and balcony. All 80 rooms have bathrooms, there is a roof terrace for sunbathing and a penthouse restaurant.

✉ **Tigne Sea Front, Sliema**
☎ **336461** 🚌 **60, 61, 62, 63, 64, 67, 68 from Valletta, 70 from Buġibba, 65 from Rabat, 86 from Buġibba and Rabat, 645 from Ċirkewwa, 652 from Golden Bay**

Plaza Regency Hotel (££)

A prime location on the seafront. All the rooms have air-conditioning, the more expensive a sea view. Good middle-range establishment, classified as a three-star hotel, with a pool and restaurant.

✉ **248 Tower Road** ☎ **338408**
🚌 **60, 61, 62, 63, 64, 67, 68 from Valletta, 70 from Buġibba, 65 from Rabat, 86 from Buġibba and Rabat, 645 from Ċirkewwa, 652 from Golden Bay**

Gozo

Cornucopia Hotel (£££)

A converted farmhouse with nearly 50 rooms. There are pools, restaurants and an air of relaxed comfort. Two neighbouring farmhouses have been converted for extra accommodation and these can be rented while enjoying all the hotel facilities. Recommended.

✉ **10 Gnien Imrik Street, Xagħra, Gozo** ☎ **556486**
🚌 **64, 65 from Victoria**

Marsalforn Hotel (£)

Located close to the seafront, its 20 rooms offer economical accommodation. There is a small restaurant. Basic, clean and well-managed.

✉ **Rabat Road, Marsalforn, Gozo** ☎ **556147** 🚌 **21 from Victoria**

St Joseph's Guesthouse (£)

This tiny guest house with just 14 beds makes a pleasant overnight stay away from the tourist scene. Has its own restaurant.

✉ **131 Conception Street, Quala, Gozo** ☎ **556573**
🚌 **42, 43 from Victoria**

St Patrick's Hotel (£££)

One of the best hotels in Gozo. Half of the 49 rooms face the sea and there is a restaurant, bar, and water sports for guests' use, making this a useful base.

✉ **Xlendi, Gozo** ☎ **562951**
🚌 **87 from Victoria**

Ta'Cenc Hotel (£££)

A strong contender for the best hotel in Malta and Gozo. A tremendous location, overlooking cliffs and sea. All 83 rooms are stylishly decorated with a terrace or garden. Tennis courts, swimming pools and a private rocky beach with its own restaurant/bar. Includes stone-built *trulli* bungalows with beehive roofs.

✉ **Sannat, Gozo** ☎ **556819**
🚌 **52 from Victoria**

Three Hills Guest House (£)

Not a lot of choice in Victoria but this little 10-room guest house is fine for a good-value short stay.

✉ **Xagħra Street, Victoria, Gozo**
☎ **551895** 🚌 **25 from Mġarr**

Buying a Property

Non-Maltese visitors can buy and sell most types of property, over a minimum value of LM15,000, after obtaining a permit from the Ministry of Finance (☎ 236306). Only one property can be owned at any one time and the funds used to buy must be transferred from abroad. Property agents are easy to find, especially in the Sliema area.

Markets

When and Where
Shops in Malta and Gozo generally open Monday to Friday at 9AM and often close for a couple of hours in the afternoon before re-opening around 4PM and finally closing at 7PM. On Saturday shops are usually only open for the morning, but on Sunday very few open. The largest concentrations of shops are in Valletta, Sliema and Rabat.

Valletta
Open Air Markets
There are two open air markets in Valletta. Triq il-Merkanti (Merchants Street) is mostly clothes and accessories, religious icons, music cassettes, CDs and videos and there is little else of consumer interest. On Sunday a very busy market opens up in St James' Ditch, near the Triton Fountain, and although it does get frenzied at times there is also a more interesting collection of bric-a-brac, which might appeal to visitors, who will also enjoy watching the activity.

⊠ **Triq il-Merkanti (Merchants Street) and St James' Ditch, Valletta**

⊙ **Triq il-Merkanti: Mon–Sat 7–noon; St James' Ditch: Sun 6:30–1PM**

Indoor Market
Valletta's indoor market is mostly devoted to food and this is the place to visit the day before you leave Malta to make a last-minute purchase of *gbejna* (Gozitan cheese). It may not be available in sealed packets but it will keep fresh for the flight home and once put in the refrigerator the shelf life of this cheese is at least one month. The peppered version (*tal-bzar*) is recommended for those who prefer a much stronger cheese.

⊠ **Triq il-Merkanti (Merchants Street) where the open air market ends**

⊙ **Mon–Sat 6:30–PM**

Around Malta
Marsaxlokk Open Air Market
Basically a fish market, it is still very interesting to see for those who are not actually making a purchase. The variety of shapes and colours of the Mediterranean fish here is surprising, making an attractive scene; and what you see here may well end up on your own plate when you visit one of Marsaxlokk's many very excellent fish restaurants.

⊠ **Along the water front, Marsaxlokk**

⊙ **Sun 7–11:30AM** 🚌 **27 from Valletta, 427 from Bugibba, 627 from Paceville**

Other Open Air Markets
Many towns in Malta have an open air market once or twice a week and they are worth visiting if you are in the area, but do not go out of your way to make a special trip. They are not tourist markets, but they do provide a welcome opportunity to mix with Maltese people going about the business of shopping.

⊠ **Birkirkara, near the Church of St Helen**

⊙ **Wed, Fri 7–11AM**

🚌 **41, 42, 71, 78**

⊠ **Birżebbuġa, in St Catherine Street near the Government Primary School**

⊙ **Thu 7–11AM**

🚌 **11, 115**

⊠ **Naxxar, 21st September Ave**

⊙ **Thu 7–11AM**

🚌 **54, 55, 56, 65**

⊠ **Rabat, opposite St Paul's Parish Church**

⊙ **Sat 7–11AM**

🚌 **80, 81, 83, 84, 86, 65**

⊠ **Vittoriosa, St Margherita Heights**

⊙ **Tue 7–11AM**

🚌 **1, 2, 4, 6**

Handicrafts, Arts & Antiques

Valletta

Artisans Centre

A few doors away from the tourist information office is one of the best shops for a general selection of quality handicrafts. The jewellery section has handsome Maltese crosses on chains. Picture frames, prints, souvenirs and gifts are also available.

✉ **9 and 10 Freedom Square, Valletta** ☎ **246216** ⏰ **Mon–Fri 9–1, 4–7; Sat 9–1**

Galea Paintings

The studio and gallery of the artist Aldo Galea. The subject is Malta, especially shipping scenes. The work sells for between LM15 and LM150. A posting and packing service can also be arranged.

✉ **8 Merchants Street, Valletta** ☎ **243591** ⏰ **Mon–Fri 3:30–7; Sat 9:15–12:45**

The Silversmith's Shop

The shop is wallpapered with postcards sent by satisfied customers from around the world and this now seems to be an essential belated part of any transaction! A fair selection of chains and earrings, plain and filigree, and the silversmith is usually busy at work over a small table in the middle of the shop.

✉ **218 Republic Street, Valletta** ☎ **231416** ⏰ **Mon–Fri 9–6; Sat 9–1**

La Valette Art Gallery

Original prints, antique engravings, oil paintings and maps at reasonable prices. Hand-coloured prints of Malta are based on old originals, and some interesting oil and tempura miniatures are hand-painted on copper plates.

✉ **3b Strait Street, Valletta** ☎ **222330** ⏰ **Mon–Fri 10–1, 5:30–7; Sat 10–12:30**

Around Malta

Empire Arts and Crafts Centre

This huge crafts emporium sells just about everything. The lace work, paintings, glass and ceramics take second place to the largest selection of jewellery in Malta. Necklaces, brooches, earrings, bangles and talismans are here, plus an astounding variety of watches. Craftspeople make lace, glass and silver filigree; cafeteria. Highly recommended.

✉ **20A/B St Agatha Street, Rabat** ☎ **453245** ⏰ **Mon–Sat 10–6** 🚌 **80, 81, 83, 84, 86**

Galleria Cremona

Marco Cremona is a Maltese artist, born in 1951, who studied in Italy and London and worked as an art teacher before turning professional. His paintings have been exhibited in Europe and his work, usually impressions of Malta, sells for between LM75 and LM500; prints are a lot less expensive.

✉ **16 Museum Road, Rabat** ☎ **450509** ⏰ **Summer: Mon–Sat 10–6** 🚌 **80, 81, 83, 84, 86**

Mdina Glass

Decorative glass is made in the traditional manner by hand and mouth; also etching and crystal cutting.

✉ **Ta' Qali Craft Village, Ta' Qali** ☎ **415786** ⏰ **Jun–Oct, Mon–Fri 8–6; Sat 8–12:30. Nov–May: Mon–Fri 8–4; Sat 8–12:30** 🚌 **80 from Valletta or Rabat**

What to Buy

Maltese handicrafts are the best items to take home. Apart from the glass, choose from filigree silver jewellery, Maltese crosses, gold jewellery, lace work and ceramics. Italian clothes tend to predominate in the boutiques in Sliema.

Glass

One of the best buys is glass and there are three main types. The blue and green Mdina glass is probably the most widely distributed in shops and it can be seen being made at Ta' Qali (► below). Phoenician glass, a characteristic deep blue, is made on Manoel Island (► 50) and is also available in good shops. Vibrantly coloured Gozo glass, the most expensive, is best purchased on Gozo (► 107).

Melitensia Art Gallery

This is regarded as one of the best art galleries in Malta, and a trip here could be combined with a visit to the nearby San Anton Gardens (► 44).

🖂 Vjal it-Trasfigurazzjon (Transfiguration Ave), Lija ☎ 430338 ⏰ Mon–Fri 10–1, 4–7; Sat 10–1 (or by private appointment) 🚌 40

Phoenician Glassblowers

The workshop studio is on Manoel Island and a free boat service is available from The Strand in Sliema. The beautiful blues and yellows of the glass are many visitors' favourites.

🖂 Manoel Island, Gzira ☎ 313606 ⏰ Mon–Sat 9–4:30 🚌 60, 61, 62, 63, 64, 67, 68 from Valletta, 70 from Rabat, 65 from Buġibba and Rabat, 86 from Buġibba and Rabat, 645 from Ċirkewwa, 652 from Golden Bay 🚢 Valletta–Sliema ferry (☎ 335689)

Ta' Qali Craft Village

The site is a disused airfield from World War II and the crews' Nissen huts are now devoted to the peaceful business of retailing lace, glass and other crafts. Mdina Glass have their workshop here.

🖂 Ta' Qali ☎ 415786 ⏰ Mon–Fri 8–6; Sat 8–12:30

Tres Chic Antique Gallery

Antiques from the Mediterranean, as well as Britain and Ireland.

🖂 Main Street, Mosta ☎ 417305 ⏰ Mon–Sat 9:30–noon, 4:30–7 🚌 43, 44, 45, 49, 53, 56, 57

Village Crafts

This tiny shop is a few doors down from McDonald's. It specialises in handcrafted crochet lace with a surprisingly wide range for such a small space.

🖂 30A St George's Road, St

Julian's ☎ 338151 ⏰ Mon–Sat 9–1, 3:30–10 🚌 62, 64, 67, 68, 70 from Valletta, 627 between Paceville and Marsaxlokk

Welcome to the Lace Shop

This small shop situated near St Paul's in Rabat is packed with lace tablecloths and matching napkins. Most is hand-made but there is also some less expensive machine-made lace.

🖂 5 Triq San Kataldu, Rabat ☎ 454290 ⏰ Mon–Fri 9:30–5; Sat 9:30–3:30 🚌 80, 81, 83, 84, 86

Gozo

Bastion Lace

More than one little shop sells handicrafts in the Citadel, but only attractive hand-made lace is sold in this delightfully tiny shop. Friendly service, no undue pressure to buy.

🖂 Bieb l-Imdina Street, Citadel, Gozo ☎ 561471 ⏰ Mon–Sat 9:30–5

Gozo Antiques

Plates, clocks and mirrors account for some of the more portable merchandise. The shop does not arrange shipping, so there is a limit to what can easily be taken home in your luggage.

🖂 35 Enrico Mizzi Street, Victoria, Gozo ☎ 562422 ⏰ Mon–Fri 4–7 🚌 25 from Mġarr

Gozo Glass

The glass-making workshop is on show inside the shop. Some people find Gozo glass gaudy and flashy, but there are beautiful examples to be found here, and a visit is recommended. The shop is on the main road just outside Gharb on the road to Victoria.

🖂 Triq l-Gharb, Gozo ☎ 561974 ⏰ Mon–Sat 9–6 (Workshop closes at 3:30, Sun 10–4) 🚌 2, 91

Ta' Dbiegi Craft Village

Heading west from Victoria, take the left fork after passing the turn-off for Ta' Pinu Church. The craft village is on the left of the main road before reaching San Lawrenz. There is nothing craft like about the premises: characterless low-level British military huts converted into shops. Pottery, art, lace and clothes account for most of the merchandise.

⊠ **On the main road between Ta'Pinu Church and San Lawrenz** ☎ **556202**
🕐 **Daily 8:30–6:45**
🚌 **2, 91 from Victoria**

Joe Xuereb

Hand-carved and hand-decorated sculptures using Gozo stone. The best pieces look as if they might be thousands of years old, and not cheap. Situated in the village of Għajnsielem, reached by turning right into Għajnsielem Street from the main road to Victoria shortly after leaving the ferry at Mġarr.

⊠ **Ta' Peppi, Bahhara Street, Għajnsielem, Gozo** ☎ **553559**
🕐 **Daily 10–4**

Souvenirs

Valletta
Asia

Decorative boxes, plates, candle holders, pottery and gifts from a small chain of shops.

⊠ **24 St Lucia Street, Valletta** ☎ **239207** 🕐 **Mon–Fri 9–1, 4–7; Sat 9–1**

Gopaldas Oriental Bazaar

Two floors of gifts from Malta and the Orient. There is little of real quality but for inexpensive souvenirs and gifts the place is worth a quick browse.

⊠ **33 Republic Street, Valletta** ☎ **224938** 🕐 **Mon–Sat 9:30–7; Sun (Apr–Oct) 10–1**

Around Malta
Ceramica Saracina

The colourful bowls and plates with pastoral designs in this pottery shop make a pretty gift or just something to keep and remind you of your trip to Malta.

⊠ **87 St Anthony Street, Attard** ☎ **440976** 🕐 **Mon–Fri 8:30–5:30; Sat 8:30–1** 🚌 **40**

Mdina Souvenirs

Old coins, glass, prints and lace, including a good selection of hand-made brass door knockers. This little shop also hires out multilingual audio guides with a map to facilitate one's walkabout in Mdina.

⊠ **1 St Publius Square, Mdina** ☎ **415436** 🕐 **Mon–Sat 9–5 (occasional Sun in Jul, Aug)**
🚌 **80**

Stockhouse

There are souvenirs galore plus gifts in this popular, inexpensive tourist shop. There are also knitted woollen garments for sale for those who can overcome the psychological barrier of contemplating them when the island's heat is ferocious.

⊠ **Islets Promenade, Buġibba** ☎ **571554** 🕐 **Mon–Sat 9–10; Sun 9–1** 🚌 **49 from Valletta, 48 from Ċirkewwa, 51 from Għajn Tuffieħa, 70, 645, 652, from Sliema, 86 between Buġibba and Rabat, 427 between Buġibba and Marsaxlokk**

Gozo
Cittadella Centre

Situated just off Victoria's main square, this shopping mall has stores devoted to perfume, jewellery, lace, clothes, leather, glass, ceramics and gifts. There is also a restaurant, bar, cafeteria and ice-cream parlour for that much-needed refreshment break.

⊠ **14-16 Sir Adrian Dingli Street, Victoria, Gozo** ☎ **556628** 🕐 **Mon–Sat 9–5** 🚌 **25 from Mġarr**

Lace

Gozo is renowned for its hand-made lace, a traditional home-based activity that began life as a devotional act by pious women making lace adornments for their local church. Shawls and tablecloths are the most popular items and prices are reasonable. Rabat in Malta and the Citadel in Gozo are the best places to make a purchase.

Dinosaurs, Dungeons, Leisure Parks & Rides

Multi-Media Events

Older children should enjoy some of the multi-media 'experiences' (► 110). They manage to be educational as well as entertaining, and the souvenir shop at the Malta Experience could empty purses of pocket money. The Wartime Experience (► 41) is best reserved for teenagers.

Although the Mediterranean Sea is all around, Malta does not have many sandy beaches. The two most popular ones – Mellieha Bay, and Għajn Tuffieħa – tend to be crowded, but that rarely bothers children and is often an asset. Swimming off the rocks is not suitable for young children and it is better to stick with the hotel pool or lido. The St Julian's area is best for lidos, there being one on the main road (Club Neptune, see below) and another at the San Gorg Corinthia Hotel (► 101).

Club Neptune

A waterpolo and swimming club open to non-members on a daily membership basis. The fresh-water pool is heated and there are restaurant and bar facilities. It is located near the Barracuda restaurant on the waterfront, and parents might wish to retire across the road to the City of London café and bar while their children frolic.

🖂 **Balluta Bay, Street Julian's** ☎ **No tel** 🕓 **Daily 8–5** 🚌 **62, 64, 67, 68, 70 from Valletta, 627 between Paceville and Marsaxlokk**

Dinosaurs

Perhaps the best thing about these life-sized reproductions enhanced by animation, sound and lighting is their location close to the Mdina Glass factory and other craft shops. Children should also enjoy the glass-blowing (► 105).

🖂 **Ta' Qali National Park, Ta' Qali** ☎ **416720** 🕓 **Jun–Sep: Mon–Sat 10–6. Oct–May: daily 11–4** 🚌 **80 from Valletta or Rabat**

Eden Super Bowl and Cinemas

A computerised bowling alley with 20 lanes and a bar, while both next door and across the road a huge multi-cinema complex combine to make this an evening's entertainment for the young. The Paceville location means plenty of fast-food type restaurants within walking distance.

🖂 **Paceville, St George's Bay** ☎ **319888** 🕓 **Daily 10AM– 12:30AM** 🚌 **62, 64, 67, 68, 70 from Valletta, 627 between Paceville and Marsaxlokk**

Helicopter Ride

One possibility is to combine transport with pleasure and take the children to and from Gozo via helicopter, departing from Malta's international airport and arriving at the Xewkija heliport in Gozo. Fare for children under 12 is 50 per cent of the fare adult. Discount for students with a student card. Sightseeing helicopter flights lasting either 20 or 40 minutes are also available.

🖂 **Malta Aircharter, Luqa** ☎ **662211 (Air Malta), 557905 (Gozo Heliport), 243777 (Valletta), 330646 (Sliema)** 🕓 **Daily**

Mdina Dungeons

Pass through Mdina Gate and these medieval dungeon chambers are immediately on one's right: 'Discover Horror, Drama and Mysteries from the dark past'. Young children will love the waxwork scenarios and their gruesome details.

🖂 **Street Publius Square, Mdina** ☎ **450267** 🕓 **Jun–Sep: 10–7. Oct–May: 10–6** 🚌 **80, 83, 86**

Mistra Village

In nearly all the better and bigger hotels the needs of children are well-provided for and there is usually a children's pool. The Mistra Village tourist village deserves first prize in this respect (➤ 102). Non-residents may leave their children at an animation show plus disco in the evening, while enjoying a meal in the hotel restaurant, and then join the children later for a show and disco in the amphitheatre.

✉ Xemxija Hill, Street Paul's Bay ☎ 580481 🚌 43, 44, 45, 50, 51, 52

Playmobil FunPark

The German lego-like toy company has a shop, play area and water channels to amuse young children. Tours of the toy factory are sometimes available but telephone ahead to check.

✉ B36 Bulebel Industrial Estate, Żejtun
☎ 693763 🕐 Jul–Sep: Mon–Fri 9–6; Sat 6–9pm. Oct–Jun: Mon–Fri 9–5:30
🚌 27, 28, 29, 30 Sweethaven/ Popeye Village ➤ 73

Splash and Fun Park

On the main road between Sliema and Buġibba, this water-based leisure park has colour-coded water chutes (yellow for the recklessly brave, blue for the not so daring and white for everyone else), a lagoon pool and a dinosaur theme park. There is also a snack bar and a pool-side barbeque at weekends.

✉ White Rocks, Bahar ic-Caghaq
☎ 374283
🕐 Daily 9–6
🚌 70 from Sliema or Buġibba, 68 from Valletta

Sun City

A new leisure centre in Marsaskcala comprising four cinemas, the jazzy Carry on Dining restaurant with neon-lit pop posters on the walls, the Casablanca cafeteria with a bar, an ice-cream parlour and a sweet shop.

✉ Triq Il-Gardiel, Marsakcala
☎ 632858
🕐 Daily 10–2, 6:30–11 (later closing summer weekends)
🚌 19, 20, 22

Toys Museum

There is little in Gozo that is specifically aimed at children but that is not a reason for thinking of not visiting the island with young ones. The journey there, by boat or helicopter (➤ 108), is pleasantly short and interesting and once on Gozo the Citadel at Victoria has plenty of museums (➤ 84) suitable for children. There is a Toys Museum in Xagħra for younger children. The Gozo 360° audio-visual show on the history and culture of Gozo (➤ 111) is another possibility.

✉ Xagħra, Gozo ☎ 562489
🕐 Mon–Sat 10–12, 3–6 🚌 64, 65 from Victoria

Underwater Safari

Children should enjoy a trip in MV Seabelow's observation keel, for it is below the level of the sea with windows for viewing marine life, including the odd passing octopus. The boat has a feed-ing system that keeps fish in its vicinity so there is always something to see amidst the algae. Every passenger has at least 20 minutes in the observation keel during the one-hour trip.

✉ Captain Morgan Cruises, Dolphin Court, Tigne Seafront, Sliema ☎ 343373
🕐 Dep from Sliema and Buġibba from 10AM onwards
🚌 Sliema: 60, 61, 62, 63, 64, 67, 68 from Valletta, 70 from Bugibba, 65 from Rabat, 86 from Buġibba and Rabat, 645 from Čirkewwa, 652 from Golden Bay Buġibba; 🚢 Valletta-Sliema ferry (☎ 335689)

Discotheques

The usual pattern for Malta's discos is to allow people in for free before about 10PM and until at least 11PM there are few people over 21 on the dance floor. This makes them ideal for teenagers who can safely enjoy the sound and lighting effects and the videos. (➤ 113 for details of the more popular discos).

Trips & Shows, Casinos & Cruises

A Day Trip to Sicily

Various tour companies offer a one-day trip to Sicily that includes the return trip by catamaran and a coach tour to Mt Etna and other places of interest. Departure is usually around 7AM, returning to Malta around 11PM. Do not forget your passport.

Valletta

The Malta Experience

If time and inclination restrict you to visiting just one of the multilingual audio-visual, large-screen presentations about Malta and Gozo then this is the one to see. The theatre is set inside the historic 16th-century Sacra Infermeria (► 40) and the show sets itself the daunting task of presenting Malta's history from Neolithic times onwards in 50 minutes. With the help of 3, 000 colour slides and 39 projectors it does this well. There is access for visitors with disabilities and there is also a restaurant and souvenir shop.

🖾 **Sacra Infermeria/ Mediterranean Conference Centre, end of Merchants Street near Fort Street Elmo, Valletta**
☎ **243776**
🕐 **Mon–Fri on the hour 11–4; Sat-Sun 11–1PM**

Sacred Island

This audio-visual presentation focuses on the role of religious faith in the history of Malta, from the fertility gods of prehistoric times to the visit of Pope John Paul II in 1990. In between, St Paul, the catacombs, the Knights, Mdina religious art and festas all get a mention. A joint ticket is available for Sacred Island, St John's Co-Cathedral Museum and Mdina Cathedral Museum.

🖾 **Upper Barrakka Hall, Dar l-Emigrant, Valletta**
☎ **222644** 🕐 **Mon–Fri 10, 11:30, 1PM, 2:30, 4; Sat 10, 11:30, 1;Sun 10, 11:30**

The Valletta Experience

This multi-media show is shown in the same building as the Wartime Experience (► 41) and a combined ticket offers a small saving. The 45-minute show covers the history, legends and folklore of the capital and the highlight for most viewers is the sequence covering the Great Seige. If you like those kinds of shows then you will enjoy this, but it still ranks third place after the Malta Experience and the Wartime Experience. There is no wheelchair access. A small bar downstairs serves drinks and snacks.

🖾 **Civil Service Sports Club, Palace Square** ☎ **247891**
🕐 **Mon–Fri 10, 12, 2; Sat 10 and 12**

Around Malta

The Casino

Malta's state-owned casino, the Dragonera Palace, has a terrific location on a promontory overlooking St Jeagis Bay, and, if you can be sure of limiting your risk, a visit is recommended; the next closest casino is actually in Tunisia.

There are tables in the Gaming Hall for roulette, blackjack and *chemin-de-fer* as well as slot machines and video poker machines. Roulette is the most popular because the rules are easy to follow; there is a free explanatory booklet for all the games. The minimum and maximum bets on a single roulette number are LM 1 and 10 respectively. There is a bar and restaurant, and a dress code requiring a jacket and tie (these may be borrowed at the entrance, supply permitting). An adjoining building, Slots Palace, is devoted solely to slot machines. There is no dress code here but is has absolutely none of the casino atmosphere either, rather it just appeals to the fairly dedicated gamblers who are attracted by the LM 5,000 jackpot.

🖂 **Dragonara Palace, St Julian's** ☎ 344550
🕐 **8:30–4PM** 🚌 **62, 64, 67, 68, 70 from Valletta, 627 between Paceville and Marsaxlokk**

Grand Harbour Cruise
Captain Morgan, a well-established Maltese tour company, offers a popular lunchtime buffet harbour cruise that departs daily from Sliema and tours both the Grand Harbour and Marsamxett Harbour. There is a running commentary on the history of the area before docking at Senglea (➤ 70) for an hour's free walkabout and then returning to Sliema. The price of the trip includes a hot and cold buffet and also wine.

🖂 **Captain Morgan Cruises, Dolphin Court, Tigne Seafront, Sliema** ☎ 343373
🕐 **Departs at 11AM, returns 3PM. Dec–Feb: Tue, Thu only)**
🚌 **60, 61, 62, 63, 64, 67, 68 from Valletta, 70 from Buġibba, 65 from Rabat, 86 from Buġibba and Rabat, 645 from Ċirkewwa, 652 from Golden Bay** ⛴ **Valletta-Sliema ferry (☎ 335689)**

The Mdina Experience
An audio-visual, multilingual spectacular spanning some 3,000 years of Mdina's history in half an hour. This is presented in a suitably ancient building. The presentation covers the Roman and Arab periods of occupation, the Knights of Malta, French and British rule. There is a coffee shop and a gift shop with an array of souvenirs. The 30-minute programme runs continuously every half an hour during the opening times below.

🖂 **7 Mesquita Square, Mdina**
☎ **454322** 🕐 **Mon–Fri 11–4:30;**

Sat 11–1:30 🚌 **80, 83, 86 from Valletta, 65 from Sliema**

Gozo
Boat Trips
Pleasure trips lasting over six hours and circling the island depart from Marsalforn. The trip takes in the Azure Window in the morning, before anchoring in Xlendi Bay for lunch and proceeding south via the Ta' Ċenċ cliffs and on to Comino and the Blue Lagoon. A similar trip does the journey in the opposite direction from Xlendi and there are also trips that spend more time on Comino, and an itinerary to Popeye Village in Malta.

🖂 **Xlendi Pleasure Cruises,**
☎ **555667 (Marsalform), 562548 (Xlendi)** 🕐 **Dep 11, return 5:30**
🚌 **21 from Victoria for Marsalforn; 87 for Xlendi**

Gozo 3600
Not to be outdone by similar shows in Valletta and Mdina, Gozo now has its very own sound-and-vision show designed to bring the smaller island's own culture and history to life. The presentation lasts just under half an hour with a multi-lingual commentary.

🖂 **Castle Hill, Rabat, Gozo**
☎ **559955** 🕐 **Mon–Sat: every hour between 10:30 and 4:30; Sun every hour between 10:30 and 1:30** 🚌 **25 from Mġarr**

Sunset Cruise
The boat leaves Mġarr in the evening and the first port of call is Comino. Gozo cheese and *hobz biz-zejt* (bread with oil, pulped tomato, olives and seasonings) are one way to keep hunger pangs at bay as the boat proceeds to Popeye Village in Malta, and then to Comino where it anchors for dinner.

🖂 **Frankie's Gozo Diving Centre** ☎ **551315**
🕐 **Dep 6PM, return 11PM**
🚌 **25 from Victoria**

Manoel Theatre
An opportunity to catch a performance at the Manoel Theatre (➤ 39) should be seized because, whatever the actual show, just sitting in the theatre for a live performance is an experience in itself. The tourist office in Valletta will have details of any piano recital, orchestral concert or theatre that is taking place.

Bars & Discos

Bars and Pubs

The British influence means that pubs are not uncommon in Malta or Gozo and there is tremendous variety in the kind of entertainment they offer. The smallest village is likely to have a tiny bar where visitors are welcome but the only diversion will be a conversation with fellow customers. Valletta's nightlife is non-existent, so for bright lights and live music head for Paceville or Buġibba.

Bars

Malta

B.J.s

This pub has a soul. There is a small stage for bands, often very good, and usually a pleasant upbeat atmosphere despite the dark and smoky interior. Jazz evenings featured. Recommended.
✉ **Ball Street, Paceville, St Julian's** ☎ 337642 ◉ **Daily: 7–late** 🚌 **62, 64, 67, 68, 70 from Valletta, 627 between Paceville and Marsaxlokk**

Easy Rider

This energetic pub, characterised by lurid strip lighting, has two bars. One has a pool table for informal drinks and play while the larger bar pulsates to the sound of loud music and DJs from London. Mixed clientele, from mid-20s.
✉ **Dragonara Road, Paceville, St Julian's** ☎ 345204 ◉ **Daily: 6:30PM–4AM** 🚌 **62, 64, 68, 70 from Valletta, 627 between Paceville & Marsaxlokk**

Irish Pub

This Irish theme pub is part of Hotel Bernard, situated close to the Eden bowling and cinema complex. Live bands perform most nights.
✉ **St George's Bay, St Julian's** ☎ 373900 ◉ **Daily 11–2, 6.30–2AM** 🚌 **62, 64, 67, 68, 70 from Valletta, 627 between Paceville and Marsaxlokk**

Memories

Tucked away down a side-street, the two floors are popular with locals and visitors of all ages. Karaoke sometimes takes over one floor.
✉ **4 Gort Street, Paceville, St Julian's** ☎ 338778

◉ **Mon–Sat 9AM–2AM; Sun 6PM–2AM** 🚌 **62, 64, 67, 68, 70 from Valletta, 627 between Paceville & Marsaxlokk**

Saddles Pub

This pub has been around for a long time and, as one of the photographs on the wall makes clear, was once very popular with the British army. Still lively with a good atmosphere and there is an Internet wine bar on the first floor.
✉ **G. Borg Olivier Street, St Julian's** ☎ 339993 ◉ **Daily: 9–3AM** 🚌 **62, 64, 67, 68, 70 from Valletta, 627 between Paceville & Marsaxlokk**

Summer Nights

Situated on the waterfront with tables outside on the pavement and a CD jukebox inside that is wired up to an excellent sound system.
✉ **Marina Street, Marsascala** ☎ 632528 ◉ **Daily: 6PM–1AM** 🚌 **19, 22**

Zanzi Pub

Situated next to St George's Park Complex this pub opens in the morning for hot snacks at outside tables and goes through to 4AM the next morning, becoming increasingly lively as the night develops. Live music every night, including karaoke, and popular with visitors of all ages.
✉ **Dragonara Road, Paceville, St Julian's** ☎ 375443 ◉ **9:15–4AM** 🚌 **62, 64, 67, 68, 70 from Valletta, 627 between Paceville & Marsaxlokk**

Gozo

Il-Kartell

One of the more popular little bars in Marsalforn and a lively enough place as the night wears on. There is a billiards table and, although there is only taped music, sitting on the balcony and sipping drinks in this picturesque fishing village is a pleasant way to spend an evening.

✉ **Marsalforn waterfront** ☎ **556918** 🕐 **8:30PM–1AM** 🚌 **21 from Victoria**

Tapie's Bar

This little bar in Victoria's main square has a few tables outside on the street where one can idle the time away at the relaxing pace of Gozitan life.

✉ **Pjazza San Frangisk, Victoria, Gozo** 🕐 **Daily: 7–1, 4–11** 🚌 **25 from Mġarr**

Discos

Malta

Axis

Once a trendy disco and may be so again, for Paceville disco-goers shift their allegiance according to the perceived vogue. The dance floor is small but the bar area accommodates more spectators and encourages mingling.

✉ **Triq San Gorg, St Julian's** ☎ **373830** 🕐 **8–4AM** 🚌 **62, 64, 67, 68, 70 from Valletta, 627 between Paceville & Marsaxlokk**

Bar Bamboo

Opposite the new Westin hotel and with four giant multi-coloured parrots perched outside, it is not easily missed. There are indoor and outdoor bars, lively but not boisterous.

✉ **1 Dragonara Road, St Julian's** ☎ **375331** 🕐 **Winter: Daily 10AM–4AM Summer: Wed, Fri–Sat 6–late.** 🚌 **62, 64, 67, 68, 70 from Valletta, 627 between Paceville & Marsaxlokk**

Beachclub

Familiarly known as Tony and Marlyne's place, this relaxed, friendly establishment has dancing every night to CDs and a family atmosphere.

Children are welcome.

✉ **Triq Daliet, Marsaskala** ☎ **616288** 🕐 **Summer: daily 8–late; Winter: Wed–Sun 8–late** 🚌 **19, 22**

The Black Rose

The New Dolmen Hotel hosts one of the most popular late-night dancing scenes.

✉ **New Dolmen Hotel, Qawra** ☎ **581510** 🕐 **Daily 8–late** 🚌 **48, 49, 51, 70**

Euphoria

Very popular, there are four dance areas on different levels and the music varies from hip-hop to jazz to the current Top 40.

✉ **Triq San Gorg, St Julian's** ☎ **341173** 🕐 **Tue–Fri 10PM–6AM; Sat–Sun 7PM–6AM** 🚌 **62, 64, 67, 68, 70 from Valletta, 627 between Paceville & Marsaxlokk**

Reeds

This popular open-air disco in Marsaskala is on the road to St Thomas Bay.

✉ **Triq Il-Gardiel, Marsaskala** ☎ **684482** 🕐 **Fri–Sun 8–late** 🚌 **19, 20, 22**

Tremors

Popular Paceville disco, with free entry before 10AM and under 18s until after mid-night. Regular theme nights.

✉ **St George's Road, St Julian's** ☎ **337644** 🕐 **Mon–Fri 8PM–4AM; Sat–Sun 7PM–4AM** 🚌 **62, 64, 67, 68, 70 from Valletta, 627 between Paceville & Marsaxlokk**

Gozo

La Grotta

Not the most advanced sound system, but this open-air disco is delightful. Lovely views and a pub two minutes away. Opens at 11PM but comes alive well into the next morning.

✉ **Xlendi Road, Xlendi, Gozo** ☎ **551149** 🕐 **11PM–6:30AM** 🚌 **87 from Victoria**

Buġibba Bars

The place to be for young folk in Buġibba is where Pioneer Road meets the promenade. A cluster of popular bars and numerous eating places nearby makes this a natural meeting place and drinkers from pubs like the Bonkers, Coconut Creek, and the Victoria spill outside and loudly share the pavement.

Sports

Health CLubs
A number of the better hotels have health and leisure clubs and some of them can boast excellent facilities. The Apollo Club at the San Gorg Corinthia (☎ 374114) includes a computerised system that produces a fitness profile and the Jerma Palace (☎ 633222) has superb facilities.

Athletics

The Malta Amateur Athletics Association
It is worth contacting to see what events are being organised during the time of your stay. Cross-country and track-and-field events are held fairly regularly.
✉ Brantwood, A/6 Main St, Mosta ☎ 411910 🚌 43, 44, 45, 49, 53, 56, 57

Bowling
For 10-pin bowling visit the Eden Super Bowl (► 108). There is a shop selling equipment, and a licensed bar.

Diving
Scuba divers are well catered for and 30- and 40-metre dives can be enjoyed with clear visibility. A useful brochure from the tourist board has a map showing the most popular dive sites and other helpful information.

The Association of Professional Diving Schools
Has details of all registered diving companies.
✉ Msida Court, 61/2 Msida Sea Front, Msida ☎ 336441

Divecare
BSAC/CMAS and PADI courses are held regularly and dive trips for qualified divers are organised twice daily. A full PADI course, involving five water training sessions and four open water dives, costs about LM 100. For about half that there is a beginner's course which includes diving but, unlike PADI, no recognised qualification is gained.

Diving courses can also be arranged through either the Comino Hotel or the Jerma Palace Hotel (► 100).
✉ St Julian's Aquatic Sports Club, G. Borg Olivier Street, St Julian's ☎ No tel 🚌 62, 64, 67, 68, 70 from Valletta, 627 between Paceville and Marsaxlokk

Gozo Diving Centre
PADI courses are available and there is also a diver training pool for beginners' courses. The same company also operates boat cruises around Gozo and Comino.
✉ Frankie's Gozo Diving Centre, Mġarr Road, Xewkija, Gozo ☎ 551315 🚌 42, 43 from Victoria

Golf
Golf was introduced to Malta by the Governor in 1888 and a nine-hole course was established in Floriana. The present 18-hole course at the Marsa Sports Club was re-grassed a few years ago and some 50 sand bunkers were added. Temporary membership at the Marsa Sports Club (► below) allows visitors to use the course and there is a useful brochure from the tourist board that describes the nine most interesting holes.

Royal Malta Golf Club
✉ Marsa Sports Club, Aldo Moro St, Marsa ☎ 230664 🚌 1, 2, 3, 4, 5, 6, 8, 11, 12, 13, 15, 18, 19, 21, 26, 29, 32, 34, 35, 36

Sports Centres

Marsa Sports Club
The island's largest sports centre, 4km south of Valletta, with Malta's only

18-hole golf course, mini golf, 18 tennis courts, 5 squash courts, billiards, fitness centre and a swimming pool. There is also a bar and restaurant. Visitors may join on a daily/weekly basis. Golf tuition is available.

⊠ **Aldo Moro Street, Marsa** ☎ 233851 ◎ **Mon–Fri 9–9; Sat–Sun 9–5** 🚌 **1, 2, 3, 4, 5, 6, 8, 11, 12, 13, 15, 18, 19, 21, 26, 27, 29, 32, 34, 35, 36**

Soccer

To say that soccer is very popular is a serious understatement, and games are mostly played between September and May. The National Stadium is the best place to view a match but games are also played elsewhere. Contact the Football Association for information.

Malta Football Association ⊠ **280 St Paul St, Valletta** ☎ **222697**

Water Sports

Sailing and Yachting

Bring your own boat or hire one, from a dinghy to an ocean-going yacht. Between Malta, Gozo and Comino there are nearly 30 anchorages and places to hire boats include Čarsamxett Harbour and Mellieha Bay. Summer sailing regattas include the Comino regatta in June and the Malta-Syracuse race for keelboats in July. The Valletta Yacht Club at Manoel Island (☎ 331131) and the West End Restaurant in St Pauls (☎ 573418) have information on the chartering of yachts. Enquire at the Malta Sailing School (☎ 338253) for dinghy and keelboat lessons. The Ramla Bay Complex (☎ 522181) has its own sailing school

and dinghy boats and speed boats may be hired.

Malta Sailing School ⊠ **21 Msida Rd, Gzira** ☎ **434115** 🚌 **60, 61, 63, 64, 66, 67, 68, 671**

Water Sports Centre

Run by the same company that operates boat trips from Marsalforn and Xlendi (see above), the Water Sports Centre has self-drive boats from 5 HP to 25 HP (120 HP with skipper), paddle boats, canoes and rowing boats. Water-skiing and windsurfing equipment is available and fishing trips may also be arranged.

⊠ **Water Sports Centre, on the seafront at Marsalforn and Xlendi** ☎ **555667 (Marsalforn), 562548 (Xlendi)** 🚌 **21 from Victoria for Marsalforn; 87 for Xlendi**

Water Skiing

The West End restaurant in St Paul's Bay is one place to contact for water skiing and boat hire in the St Paul's Bay area. Motor boats and sailing boats can be hired by the hour as well as water skiing. Water skiing can also be arranged through the larger hotels at St Paul's Bay, Mellieha Bay, Sliema, St George's Bay and Golden Bay.

⊠ **West End Restaurant, St Paul's Street, St Paul's Bay** ☎ **573418** 🚌 **43, 44, 45, 49, 50 from Valletta, 48 from Čirkewwa**

Windsurfing

Windsurfing may be enjoyed at a number of hotels fronting the sheltered northern bays. The Ramla Bay Complex (☎ 522181) has excellent facilities for water sports, including windsurfing, and other possibilities include St George's Park (☎ 332312), the hotel on Comino (☎ 529821), St Patrick's (☎ 562951, Jerma.

Snorkelling and Diving

Both snorkellers and divers should fly a code-A flag or tow a surface marker buoy so as to alert speedboat traffic. All the diving schools are properly registered and employ only qualified instructors. There is a recompression chamber within St Luke's Hospital in Guardamangia (☎ 234765/234766, or 196, the emergency telephone number).

What's On When

Festas
Various aspects of a traditional *festa* will appeal to children, from the food stalls selling nougat to the colourful parades and the general carnival atmosphere. The firework displays – villagers try to out do each other – are especially dramatic and loud and to not be missed.

Public Holidays
Between May and October every town and village celebrates the feast day (*festa*) of its patron saint.

1 Jan New Year's Day

10 Feb Feast of Saint Paul's Shipwreck, Valletta

31 Mar Freedom Day Carnival

Days before Lent Two main processions take place: in Valetta and in Nadur, Gozo. Many villages celebrate.

Holy Week
Good Friday is marked by a procession through the streets of Valletta and many other towns. All places of entertainment are closed and there are pageants in Qormi, Żetjun, Rabat, Mosta and many other towns. The pageants start at about 5PM.

1 May Worker's Day

29 Jun Feast of St Peter and Paul. Parish *festa* in Nadur (Gozo)

15 Aug Feast of the Assumption. Parish *festas* in Attard, Ghaxaq, Gudja, Mgarr, Mosta, Mqabba, Qrendi, Victoria Cathedral (Gozo)

8 Sep Victory Day. Parish *festa* in Xaghra (Gozo)

21 Sep Independence Day

8 Dec Feast of the Immaculate Conception. Parish *festa* in Mellieha and Naxxar

13 Dec Republic Day

25 Dec Christmas Day

Other Parish *Festas* in Malta

Balluta	Last Sun in Jul
Balzan	2nd Sun in Jul
Birkirkara	1st Sun in Jul and 18th Aug
Birżebbuġa	1st Sun in Aug
Dingli	20 Aug
Floriana	3rd Sun after Easter
Għargħur	24th Aug or the Sun after
Gzira	4 Jun
Marsaskala	26 Jul or the Sun after
Marsaxlokk	2nd Sun in Jul
Mdina	Last Sun in Jan
Qormi	Last Sun in Jun and 3rd Sun in Jul
Rabat	1st Sun in Jul
Sliema	2nd Fri of Lent and 3rd Sun in Jul and 1st Sun in Jul and Sep and the Sun after 18 Aug
St Julian's	Last Sun in Aug
St Paul's Bay	Last Sun in Jul
Valletta	3rd Sun after Easter, 1st Sunday before 4 Aug
Vittoriosa	10 Aug or the nearest Sun
Żurrieq	1st Sun in Sep

Other Parish *Festas* in Gozo

Għarb	1st Sun in Jul
San Lawrenz	Last Sun in Jul
Sannat	4th Sun in Jul
Victoria	3rd Sun in Jul
Xewkija	4th Sun in Jun
Żebbuġ	20 Aug

Practical Matters

TIME DIFFERENCES

GMT 12 noon	Malta 1PM	Germany 1PM	USA (NY) 7AM	Netherlands 1PM	Spain 1PM
→	→	→	←	→	→

BEFORE YOU GO

WHAT YOU NEED

● Required
○ Suggested
▲ Not required

	UK	Germany	USA	Netherlands	Spain
Passport/National Identity Card	●	●	●	●	●
Visa	▲	▲	▲	▲	▲
Onward or Return Ticket	●	●	●	●	●
Health Inoculations	▲	▲	▲	▲	▲
Health Documentation (Reciprocal Agreement Document, ▶ 123, Health)	●	▲	▲	▲	▲
Travel Insurance	○	○	○	○	○
Driving Licence (national or international)	●	●	●	●	●
Car Insurance Certificate (if own car, specific to Malta)	●	●	●	●	●
Car Registration Document (if own car)	●	●	●	●	●

WHEN TO GO

Malta

▬▬▬ High season
▭▭▭ Low season

JAN	FEB	MAR	APR	MAY	JUN	JUL	AUG	SEP	OCT	NOV	DEC
15°C	15°C	16°C	19°C	23°C	28°C	30°C	31°C	28°C	24°C	20°C	17°C

 Very wet   Wet   Cloud   Sun

TOURIST OFFICES

In the UK (also responsible for Eire)
Malta Tourist Office
Malta House
36–38 Piccadilly
London W1V 0PP
☎ 0171 292 4900
Fax: 0171 734 1880

email: OFFICE.UK.
tourism.org.mt
www.tourism.org.
mt

In the USA (also Canada)
Malta National
Tourist Office
Empire State
Building, 350 Fifth
Avenue, Suite 4412
New York NY10118

☎ 212/695 9520
Fax: 212/695 8229
email: OFFICE.US.
tourism.org.mt
www.tourism.org.
mt

POLICE 191 (in Gozo: 56 20 40)

FIRE 199 (in Gozo: 56 20 40)

AMBULANCE 196 (in Gozo: 55 68 51)

AIR RESCUE: 24 43 71   SEA RESCUE: 22 50 40

WHEN YOU ARE THERE

ARRIVING

The national airline, Air Malta (☎ 69 08 90), operates scheduled flights from major European cities; there are also charter flights. Gozo has no airport. There are ferry and catamaran services from southern Italy and Sicily to Malta (Valletta). Embarkation cards to be filled in *before* passport control.

Malta (Luqa) Airport Kilometres to city centre	Journey times	
8 kilometres	🚇	N/A
	🚌	20 minutes
	🚗	15 minutes

Grand Harbour (Valletta) Kilometres to city centre	Journey times	
1 kilometre	🚇	N/A
	🚌	N/A
	🚗	2 minutes

MONEY

The monetary unit of Malta is the Maltese lira (plural: liri), which is abbreviated to LM.

The lira is divided into 100 cents (c) and there is a further subdivision of cents into mils. Though there are no longer any mil coins you may come across them in prices. Coins are in denominations of 1, 2, 5, 10, 25, and 50 cents and 1 lira and notes come in 2, 5, 10 and 20 liri.

TIME

 Malta is one hour ahead of Greenwich Mean Time (GMT+1), but from late March, when clocks are put forward one hour, to late September, Summer time (GMT +2) operates.

CUSTOMS

→ YES

Goods Obtained Duty Free (Limits for all Visitors):
Alcohol (over 22° vol): 1L *and* Wine: 1L
Cigarettes: 200 *or*
Cigarillos: 100 *or*
Cigars: 50 *or*
Tobacco: 250gms
Perfume: 'reasonable amount'
Toilet water: 'reasonable amount'
Gifts up to the value of 50 Maltese liri.

(You must be 16 and over to benefit from the alcohol and tobacco allowances.)

There are duty-free shops in the arrival and departure halls at Malta (Luqa) Airport and the Sea Passenger Terminal in Valletta.

 NO
Drugs, firearms, ammunition, offensive weapons, obscene material, unlicensed animals and certain foodstuffs.

EMBASSIES/ HIGH COMMISSIONS

UK
23 31 34/5/6
(High Commission)

Germany
33 65 31 or 33 65 20
(Embassy)

USA
24 12 40
(Embassy)

Spain
31 41 64/5/6
(Embassy)

WHEN YOU ARE THERE

TOURIST OFFICES

Malta – Head Office
● National Tourism
  Organisation
  280 Triq ir Repubblika
  (Republic Street)
  Valletta CMR02
  ☎ 22 44 44/5
  Fax: 22 04 01

**Local Tourist Information
Offices**

Malta
● 1 City Arcades
  ☎ 23 77 47

● Malta (Luqa) International
  Airport
  Arrivals Hall
  Gudja
  ☎ 24 96 00

● Main Street
  Balluta Bay
  St Julian's
  ☎ 34 26 71/2

● Bisazza Street
  Sliema
  ☎ 31 34 09

Gozo
● 1 Palm Street
  Victoria
  ☎ 55 81 06

● Mgarr Harbour
  Mgarr GSM 104
  ☎ 55 33 43

NATIONAL HOLIDAYS

J	F	M	A	M	J	J	A	S	O	N	D
1	1	(2/3)	(1)	1	2		1	2			3

1 Jan	New Year's Day
10 Feb	Feast of St Paul's Shipwreck
19 Mar	Feast of St Joseph
31 Mar	Freedom Day
Mar/Apr	Good Friday
1 May	Workers' Day
7 Jun	Sette Giugno (Commemoration of 7 June 1919)
29 Jun	Feast of St Peter and St Paul
15 Aug	Feast of the Assumption
8 Sep	Victory Day
21 Sep	Independence Day
8 Dec	Feast of the Immaculate Conception
13 Dec	Republic Day
25 Dec	Christmas Day

OPENING HOURS

○ Shops	● Restaurants
● Offices	● Museums
● Banks	● Cafés and Bars

8AM	9AM	10AM	11AM	NOON	2PM	4PM	6PM	8PM

☐ Day	☐ Mid day
☐ Evening	

In addition to the times shown above, many shops in
tourist areas stay open throughout the day. In Valletta
shops close at 1PM Saturday, and except for a few in
Buġibba, shops are closed Sunday. Offices open
earlier but do not re-open for the afternoon during the
height of summer. Banks open 8:30AM to 12:45PM in
winter. Banks also open Friday 2:30 to 4PM (4:30 to
6PM, winter) and Saturday 8 to 11:30AM (8:30AM to 12
noon, winter). Banks, businesses, shops and
museums are closed on National Holidays only.
Restaurants and bars remain open.

DRIVE ON THE LEFT

TOILETS CHARGE

PUBLIC TRANSPORT

Helicopter The fastest and most convenient way to travel between Malta and Gozo is by helicopter. The 20-seater helicopter flies between Luqa Airport (Malta) and Xewkija (Gozo) and takes 10 minutes. The operator is Malta Air Charter (☎ 66 22 11/6); departure times vary according to the season.

Trains There are no train services available on Malta or Gozo.

Cross-Island Buses Most of Malta's towns and villages are connected to Valletta by bus. Usually they depart from and return to City Gate (the main terminus). Buses (yellow with an orange stripe) are numbered but their destination is not shown, however, billboards showing the destination and route number can be found in the City Gate Bus Terminus. On Gozo, buses (grey with a red stripe) serve the main villages from Victoria but run infrequently.

Ferries Ferries from Malta to Gozo (Mġarr) depart from Ċirkewwa (20 minute-crossing) or Sa Maison (75 minutes). Services are frequent. In summer there are also passenger-only hover-marine services from Sa Maison to Mġarr (25 minutes) and from Sliema (30 minutes); some trips via the island of Comino. For information of all services (☎ 24 39 64/5/6).

Urban Transport Valletta is the only major conurbation on Malta but as driving is virtually impossible around the city most people walk. From the main bus terminus at City Gate buses are destined for other parts of the island, except for bus 98 which follows a circular route around Valletta, and is probably your best bet.

CAR RENTAL

Hire rates vary with company, group and duration, but as free mileage and insurance is included, it is cheap for Europe. Companies such as Avis (☎ 22 59 86/7/8), Europcar (☎ 23 87 45), and Hertz: (☎ 31 46 30) accept credit cards but may ask for a cash deposit.

TAXIS

Mostly white Mercedes with distinctive 'taxi' sign on roof. They do not cruise but can be picked up at the airport, harbours, by hotels, at a central rank in tourist areas, or by phone. They are fitted with meters but they are not always switched on – agree on a fare in advance.

DRIVING

Speed limits: Motorways: There are no motorways on Malta or Gozo.

Speed limits on country roads: **40mph (64kph)**

Speed limits in built-up areas: **24mph (40kph)**

Must be worn in front seats at all times and in rear seats where fitted.

Breath-testing does not take place but there are plans to introduce the practice soon.

Petrol (super grade and unleaded) is readily available. Service stations open 7AM to 6PM (4PM Saturday); some to 7PM in summer. On Sunday and public holidays a few stations open on a rota basis 8AM to 12 noon, so make sure you have enough fuel in the tank on Saturday night if planning an excursion. Petrol stations do not accept cheques or credit cards.

If you are involved in a road traffic accident, call the police immediately (☎ 191 in Malta; ☎ 56 20 40 in Gozo), and *do not* move the vehicle as it may invalidate your insurance. In the event of a breakdown there are three breakdown companies: RMF (☎ 23 54 64), MTC (☎ 32 03 49), and CAA (☎ 82 93 74). If you break down in a hired car, call the hire company to send help.

PERSONAL SAFETY

You have little to fear in Malta since the crime rate is low and the Maltese are generally honest and courteous. The police (*pulizija*) – blue uniforms similar to British police – have a station in every town and village. Report any crime to them immediately. Some precautions:

- Leave valuables in the hotel or apartment safe, not on the beach.
- Don't make yourself an obvious target for bag-snatchers or pickpockets.
- Don't leaves valuables visible in a car.

Police assistance:
☎ **191** (in Gozo: 56 20 40) **from any call box**

TELEPHONES

Malta's public telephone boxes are either green, red or see-through booths. Few phones accept coins but most take a phonecard (*telecard*) available for LM2, LM3 or LM5 from Telemalta offices, post offices, banks and news-agents. All numbers in Malta and Gozo are six-figure and there is no area code except calls from Gozo to Malta which require the prefix 8.

International Dialling Codes

From Malta to:	
UK:	**00 44**
Germany:	**00 49**
USA:	**00 1**
Netherlands:	**00 31**
Spain:	**00 34**

POST

Post Offices
There are post offices in most towns and villages. The main post offices in Merchants Street, Valletta (Malta) and 129 Republic Street, Victoria (Gozo), open later, otherwise hours are:
Open: 7:45–1:30
Closed: Sun
☎ 22 44 22 (Malta)
☎ 55 64 35 (Gozo)

ELECTRICITY

The native power supply is: 220/240 volts, 50Hz

Type of socket: 3-square-hole type taking square

plugs with 3 square pins (as used in the UK). Visitors from continental Europe should bring an adaptor; US visitors a voltage transformer.

TIPS/GRATUITIES

Yes ✓ No ✗		
Hotels (if service not included)	✓	(10%)
Restaurants (if service not included)	✓	(10%)
Cafés/bars	✓	(change)
Taxis	✗	
Porters	✓	(20c bag)
Chambermaids	✓	(50c wk)
Usherettes	✗	
Hairdressers	✓	(10%)
Cloakroom attendants	✓	(cents)

PHOTOGRAPHY

What to photograph: The natural surroundings provide some dramatic settings – spectacular pastel-coloured cliffs contrasted by rich turquoise seas.

Light: The fierce light of the midday sun should be avoided; clear early morning light or the golden light of sunset are preferable.

Film: Most well-known brands of colour print or transparency film are available but you may have difficulty finding fast-speed or black and white film.

HEALTH

Insurance

Nationals of the UK and certain other countries staying less than 30 days receive free medical treatment within the Maltese health service, but prescribed medicines must be paid for. However, private medical insurance is advised for all.

Dental Services

Dental treatment must be paid for. If you need a dentist enquire at the hotel reception desk or call directory enquiries (☎ 190 in Malta; ☎ 890 in Gozo). Private medical insurance covers dental treatment and is advised for all visitors.

Sun Advice

The Maltese Islands bask in virtual year-round sunshine; it is almost non-stop April to September. The sun is at its strongest during July and August when wearing a sunhat and covering up the skin is recommended. No topless/nude sunbathing is allowed.

Drugs

In Malta, pharmacies, usually known as chemists, are recognisable by a neon green cross sign. They sell most international drugs and medicines over the counter or by prescription. They open normal shop hours with a Sunday roster.

Safe Water

Tap water is quite safe though not very palatable. Water from fountains should be avoided as it may not come directly from the mains supply. Bottled 'table' water is available everywhere at a reasonable cost along with imported mineral water.

CONCESSIONS

Students/Youths Holders of an International Student Identity Card (ISIC) can take advantage of concessions for students including reductions of between 15 and 40 per cent on transport, exhibitions, restaurants and shops, while entrance to museums is free.

Senior Citizens Malta, a popular destination for senior citizens, offers low-cost long-stay winter packages. However, apart from a reduction on some museum fees, there are no specific discounts available.

CLOTHING SIZES

Malta	UK	Rest of Europe	USA	
46	36	46	36	Suits
48	38	48	38	
50	40	50	40	
52	42	52	42	
54	44	54	44	
56	46	56	46	
41	7	41	8	Shoes
42	7.5	42	8.5	
43	8.5	43	9.5	
44	9.5	44	10.5	
45	10.5	45	11.5	
46	11	46	12	
37	14.5	37	14.5	Shirts
38	15	38	15	
39/40	15.5	39/40	15.5	
41	16	41	16	
42	16.5	42	16.5	
43	17	43	17	
34	8	34	6	Dresses
36	10	36	8	
38	12	38	10	
40	14	40	12	
42	16	42	14	
44	18	44	16	
38	4.5	38	6	Shoes
38	5	38	6.5	
39	5.5	39	7	
39	6	39	7.5	
40	6.5	40	8	
41	7	41	8.5	

WHEN DEPARTING

- Contact the airport, airline or travel representative the day prior to leaving to ensure flights are unchanged.
- Arrive 90 minutes before your scheduled flight departure time (particularly during summer) or you may lose your flight.
- Departing visitors must complete an Embarkation Card (available at check-in area) to present at passport control.

LANGUAGE

Maltese and English are the official languages of Malta and Gozo. Almost everyone speaks English but it is Maltese that is normally heard on the streets and that predominates in the media. Maltese comprises a vast element of words of Italian, French and English origin. The alphabet consists of 29 characters: a, b, ċ (as ch in 'church'), d, e, f, ġ (as g in 'George'), g, h, ħ (as h in 'house'), i, j, k, l, m, n, għ (a single letter and usually silent), o, p, q, r, s, t, u, v, w, x, ż (as z in 'zebra') and z. Menus are all in English but road signs are for the most part in Malti. Below is a list of a few words that may be helpful.

hotel	*lukanda*	breakfast	*l-ewwel ikla tal-jum*
room	*kamra*	toilet/bathroom	*kamra tal banju*
...single/double	*singlu/doppja*	shower	*doċċa*
...one/two nights	*lejl/żewġ iljieli*	balcony	*gallarija*
...per person/per room	*kull persuna/kull kamra*	reception	*'reception'*
		key	*ċiavetta*
reservation	*riserva*	room service	*servizz fil-kamra*
rate	*rata*	chambermaid	*kamriera*

bank	*bank*	American dollar	*dollaru Amerikan*
exchange office	*uffiċju tal-kambju*	banknote	*karta tal-flus*
post office	*posta*	coin	*munita*
cashier	*kaxxier*	credit card	*karta ta' kredtu*
foreign exchange	*uffiċju tal-kambju*	cheque book	*'cheque book'*
foreign currency	*flus barranin*	exchange rate	*rata tal-kambju*
pound sterling	*lira sterlina*	commission charge	*senserija*

restaurant	*restorant*	Dinner	*ikla*
café	*café*	starter	*'starter'*
table	*mejda*	main course	*ikla*
menu	*menu*	dessert	*deserta*
set menu	*menu fiss*	drink	*xorb*
wine list	*lista ta' l-inbid*	waiter	*waiter*
lunch	*kolazjonn*	the bill	*kont*

aeroplane	*ajruplan*	ticket	*biljett*
airport	*ajruport*	..single/return	*singlu/bir-ritorn*
bus	*karozza tal-linja*	..first/second class	*l-ewwl/tieni klassi*
..station	*stazzjon tal karozza tal-linja*	ticket office	*uffiċju tal biljetti*
		timetable	*orarju*
station	*stazzjon tal*	seat	*seat/post*
ferry	*ferrovija*	non -smoking	*tpejjipx*
..terminal	*vapur terminal*	reserved	*riservat*

yes	*iva*	help!	*ajjut!*
no	*le*	today	*illum*
please	*jekk jogħġbok*	tomorrow	*għada*
thank you	*grazzi*	yesterday	*il-bierah*
hello	*merħba*	how much?	*kemm?*
goodbye	*saħħa*	expensive	*għoli*
goodnight	*bonswa*	open	*miftuħ*
sorry	*jiddispjaċini*	closed	*magħluq*

Acknowledgements
The Automobile Association wishes to thank the following libraries, photographers and associations for their assistance in the preparation of this book.
IMAGES COLOUR LIBRARY Cover (b): Valetta Street; MRI BANKERS' GUIDE TO FOREIGN CURRENCY 119; MUSEUM OF FINE ARTS VALETTA 20; PICTURES COLOUR LIBRARY Cover (c): Fishing boat; ST AGATHA'S & ST PAULS CATACOMBS 10, 15b, 24; SPECTRUM COLOUR LIBRARY 19, 46, 53; WORLD PICTURES Cover (a): Paradise Bay.
The remaining pictures are from the Association's own library (AA PHOTO LIBRARY) with contributions from: PHILIP ENTICNAP 5b, 7, 8a, 9b, 12, 13, 15a, 16, 17, 18, 21, 22, 23, 26, 27b, 30, 31, 33, 39, 42, 54, 61, 64, 68c, 71, 76, 79, 80, 84, 86, 91a, 91b, 117a; DAVID VINCENT 27a; WYN VOYSEY 1, 2, 5a, 6, 8b, 9a, 11, 25, 36, 37, 38, 40, 43, 44, 45, 49, 50, 57, 59, 60, 63, 66, 67, 68a, 68b, 69a, 70, 72a, 72b, 74, 75, 81, 83, 87, 88, 89, 90, 117b, 122a, 122b, 122c.

Author's Acknowledgements
Pat Levy wishes to thank Pat Pierce for fine-tuning the text. Thanks also to Andrew Davis at the Malta Tourist Board in London and Louis Azzopardi and Patrick Grixti at the Tourist Board in Malta. Manuel Briffa, Peter J Borg Olivier, Phillippe Lonfat and George Borg are some of the kind people in Malta and Gozo who helped; apologies to others whose names are not recorded here. A special thank you to Sean Sheehan whose contribution to the writing of this book was considerable.
The Automobile Association wishes to thank Jeffrey Mizzi and Donald Pace for their assistance.

Contributors
Copy editor: Pat Pierce Page Layout: Design 23 Verifier: Teresa Fisher
Researcher (Practical Matters): Colin Follett Indexer: Marie Lorimer

Dear Essential Traveller

Your comments, opinions and recommendations are very important to us. So please help us to improve our travel guides by taking a few minutes to complete this simple questionnaire.

You do not need a stamp (unless posted outside the UK). If you do not want to cut this page from your guide, then photocopy it or write your answers on a plain sheet of paper.

Send to: **The Editor, AA World Travel Guides, FREEPOST SCE 4598, Basingstoke RG21 4GY.**

Your recommendations...

We always encourage readers' recommendations for restaurants, nightlife or shopping – if your recommendation is used in the next edition of the guide, we will send you a *FREE* AA *Essential* **Guide** of your choice. Please state below the establishment name, location and your reasons for recommending it.

_____

_____

_____

_____

Please send me **AA *Essential*** _____

(*see list of titles inside the front cover*)

About this guide...

Which title did you buy?

AA *Essential* _____

Where did you buy it? _____

When? m m / y y

Why did you choose an AA *Essential* Guide? _____

_____

_____

_____

_____

Did this guide meet your expectations?

Exceeded ☐   Met all ☐   Met most ☐   Fell below ☐

Please give your reasons _____

_____

_____

_____

continued on next page...

Were there any aspects of this guide that you particularly liked? _____

_____

_____

_____

Is there anything we could have done better? _____

_____

_____

_____

_____

About you…

Name (*Mr/Mrs/Ms*) _____

Address _____

_____

_____ Postcode _____

Daytime tel nos _____

Which age group are you in?

Under 25 ☐   25–34 ☐   35–44 ☐   45–54 ☐   55–64 ☐   65+ ☐

How many trips do you make a year?

Less than one ☐   One ☐   Two ☐   Three or more ☐

Are you an AA member? Yes ☐   No ☐

About your trip…

When did you book? m m / y y   When did you travel? m m / y y

How long did you stay? _____

Was it for business or leisure? _____

Did you buy any other travel guides for your trip?

If yes, which ones? _____

_____

Thank you for taking the time to complete this questionnaire. Please send
it to us as soon as possible, and remember, you do not need a stamp
(*unless posted outside the UK*).

Happy Holidays!